Bafana Republic and Other Satires

A COLLECTION OF MONOLOGUES AND REVUES

Mike van Graan

WITS UNIVERSITY PRESS

Published in South Africa by:
Wits University Press
1 Jan Smuts Avenue
Johannesburg 2001

www.witspress.co.za

First published 2020

http://dx.doi.org.10.18772/32020065867

978-1-77614-586-7 (Paperback)
978-1-77614-587-4 (Web PDF)
978-1-77614-638-3 (EPUB)
978-1-77614-588-1 (Mobi)

For more information and background on the shows, including different seasons of the
shows and reviews, see www.mikevangraan.co.za. For the rights to perform the sketches
for paying audiences, contact the writer through the website.

Project manager: Lisa Compton
Copyeditor: Alison Lowry
Proofreader: Lisa Compton
Cover design: Hybrid Creative
Typeset in 10.5 point Minion Pro

Contents

Introduction

DESCRIPTION AND HISTORY

The sketches contained in this collection are derived from six different one-person satirical revues: *Bafana Republic* (2007), *Bafana Republic: Extra Time* (2008), *Bafana Republic: Penalty Shootout* (2009), *Pay Back the Curry* (2016), *State Fracture* (2017) and *Land Acts* (2018).

Except for *Land Acts*, all of these revues had their first introduction to an audience at the Franschhoek Literary Festival as part of their development.

Again, except for *Land Acts*, all the satirical revues went through a similar development process. Once I had written the script, the director would rehearse the revue with the actor for a period of three weeks, and then it would be performed at the Franschhoek Literary Festival and in other locations. Audiences were provided with one-page questionnaires through which they were invited to give feedback to each sketch – marking them out of 10, using whatever criteria they wished – with a space for further written feedback on each sketch and to the piece as a whole, including the writing, directing and acting.

As far as possible, and as part of its development, each revue would be performed for audiences that were demographically different, so that, for example, *Pay Back the Curry* was performed in the Western Cape across several venues: at the Franschhoek Literary Festival, at a private house in Kenilworth, two shows in Delft at the Rainbow Arts Foundation, at the Shack Theatre in Khayelitsha and, for a week, at the Rosebank Theatre.

After each show, I would analyse the feedback gleaned from the questionnaires. On the basis of this analysis, I would amend some sketches, even delete a few, and perhaps change the order so as to ensure a more varied emotional and entertainment journey for the audience through the course of the performance.

The long-suffering directors and actors would have to rework some of the sketches, with the actor having to unlearn many lines, and learn new ones, often before the next development show, where these changes were tested. All saw the value of the process, which, I believe, resulted in *Pay Back the Curry* achieving a rare feat at its official premiere run on the Fringe of the National Arts Festival in 2016: it sold out all 10 of its shows. Word of mouth had spread because of the development shows, and the first performance at the Festival was sold out before we arrived. The hard work of reworking scripts, with directors and actors revising the performances accordingly, paid off, as the revues were staged more competently and confidently as the development proceeded. Word of mouth continued to ensure that the shows were well attended, and audiences responded enthusiastically.

Land Acts did not go through a similar development process because I was travelling extensively before the premiere of the work at the Kalk Bay Theatre in June 2018. I was literally writing sketches while travelling and sending them to the director and actor so that they could rehearse them. By 2018 Rob van Vuuren (the director), Daniel Mpilo Richards (the performer) and I had built up a sound working relationship so that we were able to get away with this inadequate preparation on my part. I landed back in South Africa on Saturday, 2 June 2018, and the show opened on Tuesday, 5 June 2018 – my first new show where I had not seen one rehearsal before it opened!

Pay Back the Curry had two sold-out seasons at the Kalk Bay Theatre in 2016; the year after that, 2017, saw an excellent run of *State Fracture*. We had built up a solid audience for these one-person satirical revues so that by the time *Land Acts* came round, this less-developed show already had a captive audience and the revue was good enough to sell out the rest of the season.

Land Acts was also different from its predecessors in that it was produced by Daniel Mpilo Richards and myself, rather than by Siv Ngesi, who produced and essentially paid for the production costs of *Pay Back the Curry* and *State Fracture*. This foursome originally came about because Siv had commissioned me to write a stand-up show for him, which led to *Born Free*, a reflection on 20 years of democracy. However, Siv was invited to participate in the television reality show *Strictly Come Dancing* and so was unavailable to do the performance. It was then that we identified and recruited Daniel – who had graduated from drama school a year before – and he replaced Siv.

During the run of *Born Free* at Artscape's Opera Bar, it was clear that Daniel was far more talented than a stand-up comedy script allowed him to display. This led me to commit to writing a piece which would be a platform to showcase his wide array of singing, acting, accent, movement, guitar-playing and other skills. *Pay Back the Curry* was this platform, and the rest, as they say, is history.

Given the experience of *Bafana Republic*'s initial success in 2007, with Lindiwe Matshikiza, I did not expect Daniel to be available for a sequel. However, while he did receive offers to perform in other shows, Daniel chose to continue to be available to perform these one-person revues, both for the adrenalin rush of performing by oneself to a live audience, and for the greater financial rewards that one-person shows bring.

But while *Pay Back the Curry, State Fracture* and *Land Acts* represented an excellent trilogy of working relationships between the same three creatives over a period of three years, my own first forays into this genre – one-person, multi-sketch satirical revues – were quite different.

When South Africa won the bid to host the 2010 FIFA World Cup, it was highly controversial and ignited much debate about huge amounts of public funds being spent on a 'vanity project' as opposed to improving the lives of the majority of the country's citizens. I saw this as an opportunity to use sport as an entry point to make satirical commentary and to pose awkward questions about contemporary South African society. Hence the birth of the *Bafana Republic* franchise in 2007.

Lara Bye directed the highly talented Lindiwe Matshikiza in the first rendition of *Bafana Republic*, which went on to win the Best One-Person Show at the South African Comedy Awards. Spurred by the success of this revue, I was keen to write a sequel. However, Lindiwe Matshikiza was not available to do a sequel, having received invitations to undertake other work. I then decided that future sequels would serve a similar purpose – that is, they would be a platform for young actors (25 years old or younger) to showcase their talents. And each revue would have a different director.

Bafana Republic: Extra Time was performed in 2008 by Reabetswe (Rea) Rangaka, who was directed by Francois Toerien; in 2009, Lungi Pinda performed in *Bafana Republic: Penalty Shootout*, directed by Mandla Mbothwe.

I had intended to do a final revue – *Bafana Republic: Final Whistle* – to coincide with the FIFA World Cup in 2010, but didn't get around to doing so. Instead, sketches from the *Bafana Republic* franchise were stitched together thematically or otherwise for subsequent performances. For example, at the Artscape Women's Festival, Lindiwe Matshikiza performed a number of the sketches from the three revues that featured woman characters. In 2018, Daniel Mpilo Richards performed a combination of the most popular and resilient (that is, not dated) sketches from the first two shows in *Best of Pay Back the Curry and State Fracture* at the National Arts Festival; it turned out to be one of the top ticket-sellers on the Fringe that year.

WHY THE ONE-PERSON SATIRICAL REVUE FORMAT?

A revue is intended to be light entertainment, but generally includes some sharp commentary on recent events. The revue might include short plays, monologues, songs, poems, jokes, dancing and movement.

In the context of South African theatre, the one-person show is the most economically viable. It generally costs between R75 000 and R100 000 to produce a professional one-person show, with most of the expenditure (as with all theatre) taking place up front, before the show opens and begins to generate income. Three weeks of rehearsal fees for the actor and the director, hire of a rehearsal venue, designer fees, writer's fee (if the writer is not also producing), costumes, props, soundtrack, and so on all contribute to the costs, which increase exponentially with the addition of each actor.

One-person shows are also portable. We have been able to perform these revues in people's houses, traditional theatres, school halls, makeshift theatres and conference venues.

The one-person show also offers a unique platform for performers to stretch themselves, to gain confidence, to develop and consolidate their skills, and to display and celebrate their talents.

I have referred to these shows as 'satirical revues' and generally, in terms of the primary tones of each, they are. But they also include straight comedy, as well as poetry and drama which would be far more serious, taking advantage of the overall lightness of the piece to make points in more dramatic form.

One of the challenges for the performers is that it is often assumed that the material is theirs, and so they have been both complimented and criticised for it. However, the material and social commentary is mine as the writer, with the performer simply being the conduit to the audience, in much the same way as an actor will portray a character in a play whether they identify with that character or not, and unlike stand-up comedians, who generally write their own work.

In a society as polarised as South Africa's, satire provides an effective means to challenge audiences, to make them think and reflect on awkward topics, and yet to do it in a way that does not alienate them, but allows them to laugh, to be entertained and to experience a variety of emotions.

ROLES OF THE REVUES

Over the period in which these one-person shows have been performed, they have been used for a variety of purposes, including:

- raising funds for social justice and human rights NGOs;
- educating and challenging audiences, with performances followed by discussions with the audience; and
- entertainment and satirical social commentary at formal theatre spaces.

Separate sketches or collections of sketches have already been used as acting exercises, as exam performance pieces, as monologues and as performance pieces. Alternatively, a selection may be made – either along a particular theme or for the purpose of variety – to make up a show of 5 to 70 minutes. The intention with *Bafana Republic and Other Satires* is that this may continue.

The sketches are listed under the title of the original revue in which they were presented, together with the date of the revue, so that the performer, director or teacher may research the context – the collection includes some sketches that are more time-bound than others.

The sketches may also be used for in-class teaching about particular themes.

FORMS

The forms of the sketches vary according to the theme being explored and they were employed to provide variety and maintain the interest of the audience. The forms include:

- monologues, with different sketches being performed as different characters, with appropriate physicality and accents;
- duologues – conversations or exchanges between two characters, played by the same performer;
- multiple character sketches – the performer plays the role of a talk-show host interviewing a variety of characters; these may be represented as finger puppets or simply by using a different physicality and accent for each;
- poetry;
- songs;
- physical theatre; and
- stand-up comedy.

THEMES

Some of the recurring themes across the six revues are: violence against women ('Chardonnay'; 'And the Oscar goes to . . .'); corruption ('Fly SAA'; 'Saxonwold shebeen'; 'Hello, looters'; 'Ode to WaNkandla'); racism ('Dog shrink'; 'Social cohesion'; 'So-calleds'; 'Estate agent 2'); colonialism ('American and Frenchie on safari'; 'Middle finger for the natives'; 'The Helen Zille School of Good Colonialism'); and mass, premature deaths through AIDS denialism and violent crime ('Kabouter Basson'; 'A promise fulfilled').

Other themes include the polarisation of our society along racial lines and, because of poverty and inequality, the false hope projected by politicians and the wastage of resources on vanity projects – like the FIFA World Cup – when these could have spent to improve the lives of the majority of citizens.

The table provided ('Outline of sketch characters, themes, background and context') gives a useful snapshot summary.

AUDIENCE

The audience for all of the revues has generally been 'for all South Africans' (except that most of them have had an age restriction of 13 because of language and sexual innuendo). While different audiences – and different people in each audience – respond in unique ways to the sketches depending, for example, on their life experience, education, and knowledge of the politics of the day, generally the revues have worked well, generating positive feedback from high school audiences to pensioners, from males and females from Khayelitsha to Kenilworth.

PERFORMERS AND DIRECTORS

The original productions were performed and directed as follows:

Bafana Republic, 2007, performed by Lindiwe Matshikiza, directed by Lara Bye

Bafana Republic: Extra Time, 2008, performed by Rea Rangaka, directed by Francois Toerien

Bafana Republic: Penalty Shootout, 2009, performed by Lungi Pinda, directed by Mandla Mbothwe

Pay Back the Curry, 2016, performed by Daniel Richards, directed by Rob van Vuuren

State Fracture, 2017, performed by Daniel Richards, directed by Rob van Vuuren

Land Acts, 2018, performed by Daniel Richards, directed by Rob van Vuuren

AWARDS AND NOMINATIONS

Bafana Republic: Best One-Person Show, South African Comedy Awards, 2008

Bafana Republic: *Extra Time*: Best One-Person Show, South African Comedy Awards, 2009

Pay Back the Curry: Winner, Daniel Richards, Best Breakthrough Performance; Nominee, Best New South African Script, Naledi Theatre Awards, 2016

State Fracture: Winner, Daniel Richards, Standard Bank Ovation Award for Outstanding Performance, National Arts Festival, 2017

Land Acts: Winner, Daniel Richards, Best Performance in a One-Person Show; Nominee, Best New South African Script, Naledi Theatre Awards, 2019

Outline of sketch characters, themes, background and context

Sketch	Character	Theme/s	Background and context
Bafana Republic (2007)			
Interview with the CEO of the South African Football Association	White English male	The waste of resources on the 2010 FIFA World Cup	The 2010 FIFA World Cup was sold as a means for development in South Africa and Africa. This sketch explores the duplicitous purposes it actually served.
Chardonnay	'Coloured' woman at an Alcoholics Anonymous-type event	Violence against women	The violent abuse of women in South Africa is of epidemic proportions. This theme is explored through the ironic use of wine-related names.
PAHAD representative	A 'heavy' security official	Censorship	Essop Pahad was a minister in Thabo Mbeki's cabinet, known for his heavy-handed criticism of those who critiqued his boss or the political status quo.
Bhamjee	Indian businessman	Corruption in business	Abdul Bhamjee was a senior official in the South African Football Association who was convicted of fraud.
Kabouter Basson	White Afrikaans male	The number of black people who died from Mbeki's AIDS denialism	Wouter Basson was a medical doctor charged with using his medical knowledge to commit torture and murder of anti-apartheid activists. Kabouter Basson is a reference to him, but the sketch uses irony to reflect on the number of black people who have been 'killed' by the government for which they voted.

Sketch	Character	Theme/s	Background and context
Bafana Idols	Various singers	Various: Zuma's sexual escapades; Afrophobia; individual self-enrichments through the FIFA World Cup; the nostalgia of some white Afrikaans folk for a leader of the past to rescue them	Using well-known songs but changing the lyrics, this sketch uses the reality show *Idols* format to comment on different themes relevant at the time.
Bafana Republic: Extra Time (2008)			
World Cup ambassador, Hayi Buti	Ambassador to Europe, male	AIDS denialism and complicity in human rights abuses in Zimbabwe	Thabo Mbeki's presidency was marked by his AIDS denialism and by his support of Robert Mugabe, despite evidence of massive human rights abuses in Zimbabwe.
Reality show medley	Television reality show presenter	The benefits to sports administrators rather than athletes	Sports administrators and their partners were taken to international events at huge expense, while athletes received little to no funding to support their training and participation in international events.
American and Frenchie on safari	Two foreign hunters	American and European imperialism in Africa	Many European clubs buy excellent African football players; the sketch uses this as a basis to reflect on historical and contemporary neo-colonialism.

Sketch	Character	Theme/s	Background and context
AA on-screen fillers	(1) Young white Afrikaans rugby player; (2) black sportsman; (3) springbok – the animal	(1) Affirmative action; (2) substance abuse within the sports sector; (3) pressure on the national rugby symbol	(1) White people often complained about affirmative action as a strategy to correct apartheid's historical imbalances from which they benefited; (2) Ricky Januarie, a Springbok scrumhalf, was arrested for drunk driving; (3) with the springbok being inherited from the past when black people were excluded from national rugby teams, there was much debate about getting rid of the springbok as the national rugby icon.
A man's game	Child soldier	Child soldiers	With all the attention on Africa's first FIFA World Cup, this was a moment to focus on the scourge of child soldiers in some African conflicts.
ABC take-out	Child of primary school age	The burden on taxpayers to cover the costs of the FIFA World Cup	Government had to provide guarantees for the building of the stadiums required for the World Cup and general hosting of the event. This would place a burden on the national fiscus beyond the World Cup itself.
Security chief	Commander of a security firm	The 'war on terror'	After the attack on the Twin Towers of the World Trade Center in New York in 2001, major international events took additional security measures.
Bafana election fever	Television talk-show interviewer	Political party perspectives	The fourth South African elections were to be hosted in 2009, a year before the FIFA World Cup. This was an opportunity to focus on some of the differences between political parties, using the national football team as a vehicle.

Sketch	Character	Theme/s	Background and context
Vuvuzela salesman	Salesman	The waste of public resources on the 2010 FIFA World Cup	Stadiums that had been built at great expense would have ongoing maintenance costs that would be unlikely to be covered by their future use.
Whinge	Rapper/stand-up comic	Exorbitant payments to footballers in Europe and the alienation of Africans in Europe	African footballers were/are paid weekly wages in Europe that could cover the wages of hundreds of workers for a year in their country of origin. International travel is difficult for Africans, who require visas for most countries.
Stand-up comic	Stand-up comic	Things go wrong in Europe too	There were many cynics who said that South Africa, being part of Africa, would not be able to deliver a world-class event in the form of the FIFA Football World Cup.
Bafana Republic: Penalty Shootout (2009)			
Toilet cleaner	Black entrepreneur	Unrealistic expectations of enrichment through the World Cup	Toilet cleaners in airport toilets refer to the toilets as their offices which they clean for the benefit of the users and expect tips in return.
Estate agent 1	Woman estate agent	Uselessness of stadiums after the World Cup	Stadiums that had been built at great expense would have ongoing maintenance costs that would be unlikely to be covered by their future use.
False prophet	Charismatic preacher	False hope through the World Cup	Politicians sold the World Cup as 'pie in the sky', building unrealistic hope for how it would change poor people's lives.
Madonna of Africa	Celebrity musician, Madonna	Celebrity adoption of African children	Madonna went to Malawi and, controversially, adopted two children from that country.
Disabled	Disabled athlete	The need to support disabled athletes	Paralympians do better than Olympians, yet they struggle for sponsorship.

Sketch	Character	Theme/s	Background and context
Jimmy Blond	Secret agent, like James Bond	Political duplicity	A story was leaked to the media about Helen Zille having botox treatment, which was meant to embarrass her.
School for African dictators	Schoolmaster	African leadership that does not benefit their citizens	African leaders often reject criticism as imperialist intervention in their affairs, but many are responsible for gross human rights abuses.
Dog shrink	White liberal school mum	The racism of white liberals	Some formerly white schools resisted the introduction of soccer as a school sport as the demographics of the school changed.
Pay Back the Curry (2016)			
Time travel	Tour guide	Reflection on the past, the potential future and the reality of the present	People privileged by the past often expect those who were disadvantaged to 'move on' and do not want to be reminded of that past. This sketch locates the present in the context of the past, but points to a hopeful future.
Fly SAA	Female flight attendant	Corruption	Dudu Myeni, a close associate of President Zuma at the time, was the chairperson of the SAA board and allegedly facilitated much corruption in favour of the Gupta brothers and others.
Fallism	News show presenter and five student leaders	Intersectionality within the #MustFall movement	The #FeesMustFall movement played an important role in advancing free higher education, but it was wracked by internal contradictions between black consciousness, feminist and LGBTI activism.
And the Oscar goes to . . .	Presenter at film awards	Femicide	Oscar Pistorius was found guilty of killing his girlfriend, Reeva Steenkamp.

Sketch	Character	Theme/s	Background and context
Born free	Black woman student	Poverty as an obstacle to higher education and thus to social mobility	The emphasis of the #FeesMustFall movement was on free higher education; this sketch points to the need for quality education at primary and secondary levels.
Weekend special	Singer	Corruption	Using the Brenda Fassie song, this sketch comments on the appointment of Des van Rooyen as the finance minister by President Zuma, which led to the rapid decline of the rand. As a result, Van Rooyen was replaced, after a weekend in the position, by Pravin Gordhan.
I am an African	Zimbabwean poet	Afrophobia	Thabo Mbeki's 'I am an African' speech is satirised to comment on the Afrophobia of South Africans.
Estate agent 2	Woman estate agent	Racism in Cape Town	Housing for black people in Cape Town is often a site of racism, with numerous stories of how black people are prevented from renting or purchasing properties in predominantly white areas.
So-calleds	50-something 'coloured' former political activist	Black African-'coloured' racism post 1994	A trope among the 'coloured community' is that they weren't white enough for the past nor black enough for the present; this sketch reflects on the feelings of this community in the 'new South Africa'.
Blame apartheid	Singer	Using apartheid to excuse contemporary 'sins'	Irony is employed to comment on the tendency of those in power or who are accused of corruption or other crimes to blame apartheid as an excuse.

Sketch	Character	Theme/s	Background and context
The Met	Horse-racing commentator	Rivalry between political parties	Using a horse race, the sketch comments on the differences and rivalries between the main political parties.
Julius	Julius Malema	Commentary on the corruption and hypocrisy of the ruling ANC	Julius Malema was kicked out of the ANC and started the Economic Freedom Fighters, winning 25 seats in the 2014 elections. He was a thorn in the ANC's parliamentary flesh during Zuma's presidency.
Rainbow song	Singer	Rejection of the 'rainbow nation' concept	Using the song 'Somewhere Over the Rainbow', this sketch speaks to the 'rainbow nation' as a concept that excludes the poor.
State Fracture (2017)			
Saxonwold shebeen	Indian barman	Corruption – particularly as it pertains to the Gupta brothers	Brian Molefe, former head of Transnet and allegedly a chief facilitator of corruption in favour of the Gupta brothers, tried to account for his presence close to the Gupta compound by claiming that he was at a shebeen in Saxonwold.
Trumple-Thin-Skin	Story-teller	Trump's multiple madness	The sketch comments on the American president and some of his many foibles.
Chicken shite	Female chicken	Chicken dumping	Cheap chicken exports to Africa from abroad threaten the local chicken industry.
Hello, looters	Singer	Corruption	Leonard Cohen's song 'Hallelujah' is employed to show political and corruption bias in favour of the Gupta brothers.
Blacks Adopted by Whites Anonymous	Young black woman	Use of the race card to deflect criticism	Those in positions of power who are accused of crimes and mismanagement often use racial bias against them as the reason for their 'victimisation'.

Sketch	Character	Theme/s	Background and context
Pastor Hlaudi, the miracle worker	Charismatic preacher	The decline of the SABC	Hlaudi Motsoeneng's self-delusional reign at the SABC resulted in the near destruction of the public broadcaster.
ABBA medley	Singer	Corruption, and the distance of politicians from ordinary people's lives	Using various ABBA songs, this sketch comments on the tendency to try to get as rich as possible as quickly as possible; how VIP protection of politicians is different from the crime experience of ordinary South Africans; and the favouritism shown to the Guptas when their wedding plane landed at Waterkloof airforce base.
Some black lives matter	Poet	Afrophobia	Afrophobia is an ongoing form of racism in South Africa.
Stand-up on privilege	Stand-up comic	White privilege	White privilege has become part of the local political discourse in recent times; this sketch explains it, using comedy.
The Helen Zille School of Good Colonialism	Helen Zille-type school teacher	The 'benefits' of colonialism	Helen Zille tweeted about the benefits of colonialism and elicited massive criticism.
Social cohesion	Black African Romeo and 'coloured' Juliet	Black African–'coloured' racism	The tensions in the Western Cape between 'coloured' and black African communities are put under the spotlight in this sketch.
Social media rollercoaster	A rider on a rollercoaster	Polarisation on social media	Twitter and Facebook are sites of animosity, which leads to greater social divisions often along racial lines.
The patriot	Poet	How a patriot may be defined differently in different circumstances	Poetry is a powerful vehicle for expressing a range of ideas, emotions and states of being.

Sketch	Character	Theme/s	Background and context
No Zuma, no cry	Musician/singer	Corruption allegations against President Zuma	Using the Bob Marley song, this sketch points to the hope of Zuma being removed and the country changing for the better.
Land Acts (2018)			
Derya Hanekom	Tour guide	Concerns of foreign investors in the light of the land debates	Derek Hanekom was the minister of tourism, hence the name of the sketch. With unresolved policy on land, investors are taking a wait-and-see attitude.
Give me a sign, Julius	Young, highly educated business-woman	Expectations of land redistribution	Julius Malema, at the funeral of Winnie Mandela, called on 'Mama' to give them a sign to act.
Middle finger for the natives	Cowboy as per a Western movie	Colonisation	The sketch comments on how land was taken from indigenous people by colonisers.
MacDonald's farm	Singer	Lack of land reform	The ruling party has had more than 20 years to implement land reform but has done little in this regard, while many senior politicians have farms.
A promise fulfilled	Poet	Land given in death	There are many premature deaths in South Africa and those who die are given land when they are buried.
Car guard	Car guard	Homelessness	Homeless people who live on the streets try to find various ways to survive.
Australian refuge	Australian Aboriginal	High impact of crime on black South Africans	An Australian cabinet minister lobbied for Australia to provide refuge for white Afrikaans farmers in light of the 'genocide' against them; this sketch shows that, in fact, black South Africans are overwhelmingly the victims of violent crime.

Sketch	Character	Theme/s	Background and context
A dog's life	Dog	Emigration of the middle classes because of uncertainty about the land	From a pampered dog's perspective, this sketch comments on the fear of many who have houses that land reform will result in their houses being taken away without compensation.
What a wonderful world	Singer	Inequity in land ownership	The song comments on inequality directly related to who owns land and property and who does not.
Shakespeare in love	Shakespearean actor	The ease with which foreigners are able to own land in SA	Using the titles of Shakespearean plays, the sketch speaks to the ownership of land by foreigners, implying that it is easier for foreigners to own land than for many black citizens.
Ode to WaNkandla	Poet	Repudiation of those who opposed corruption	Focusing on the illegal expenditure of public resources on President Zuma's personal residence, the sketch shows how those who resisted corruption were constantly rebuffed by those in power.
Football match	Football radio commentator	Land as a political football	Parliament debated a resolution on changing the Constitution to facilitate expropriation of land without compensation, when the Constitution already allows this.
Imagine	Singer	Hope for a better future	The John Lennon song is used to imagine a future without poverty and inequality.

Glossary of terms and translations

ag	exclamation, similar to 'oh' or 'ah'
amakwerekwere (pl)	derogatory word used by black South Africans to refer to black foreigners living in South Africa
aweh	multiple meanings, but generally an informal greeting; also used, in an exclamatory or excited tone, in agreement or confirmation
befok	exciting, cool
bek	mouth (animal's); when used in context of a person, the intention is crudely derogatory
bladdy	bloody
blerrie	bloody
boer-maak-'n-plan	farmer makes a plan
boer soek 'n vrou	farmer seeks a wife (referencing the reality television show by the same name on KykNET in which unmarried farmers are matched with women 'contestants')
braai	barbecue
braaivleis	barbecue meat
bruin	brown
bruin ou	literally 'brown chap', but referencing 'coloured' people
cheeseboy/girl	a sneering, derogatory reference to someone who – unlike most poor children at school – had cheese on their sandwiches, and so thought they were better than the rest
china	friend
coconut	derogatory reference to a black or Asian person who conforms to white culture at the expense of his or her ancestral culture – the idea being that, like a coconut, the person is dark on the outside and white on the inside
dik	thick, close (as in 'close friend')
dis nie waar nie	it's not true

domkop	dumb-head
duidelik	cool, excellent (implying admiration)
Dutchman	Afrikaner; intended as an insult
eish	exclamation with multiple meanings depending on tone in which it is uttered: surprise, astonishment, agreement, disappointment, frustration
ek wil net sê	I just want to say
Engels	English
fok	fuck
fokken	fucking (adj)
gat	hole (in the sense used: arsehole)
gatsby	bread roll with fillings: can include cold meat, chips, salad
gham	derogatory word for an uncivilised 'coloured' person
hensopper	literally 'hands-upper', someone with hands raised in surrender; developed during the Boer Wars with reference to Afrikaners who surrendered to the British or went over to the British side
honky	Americanism; derogatory reference to white person
ja	yes
jirre	derived from the Afrikaans word *Here* (meaning 'God'); used as an expression denoting exasperation
jislaaik	expression of amazement
kaal	naked, bare
Kaapse Klopse	minstrel show (specific to Cape Town), with participants in groups in colourful costumes; takes place annually on 2 January
kaffir	offensive reference to a black person
kak	crap (faeces)
kanga	printed cloth, colourfully patterned, worn as casual clothing
kêrel	boy, chap; a camaraderie-type form of address
koek	cake, but also a crude reference to female genital organs
koeksiester	refers to 'koeksister', the plaited sweet pastry, but spelled incorrectly deliberately to be crude – 'koek' referring to female genital organs and 'sies' being an expression of distaste

kugel	'Jewish princess'; conscious of style, social climbing; often has a nasal twang to speech
kwaai	cool
laager	circular, protective/defensive formation for wagons; generally used to imply a protective grouping
laaitie	youngster, small boy
lanie	slang for 'sir'
lekker	nice
lobola	bride price
mal	mad, crazy
mampoer	distilled drink made from fermented fruit, with a very high alcohol content
manne	men, chaps
meisie	miss
moer	beat up
moerse	used to emphasise strong feelings
moet val	must fall
moffie	derogatory term for gay male person
mos	just
mozzie	mosquito
mugu	idiot (mildly/affectionately derogatory)
Mxit	cell-phone chat group
naai	have sex, but also a derogatory term similar to the way 'cunt' might be used (e.g. 'You are a cunt!')
nê	isn't that so?
oke	slang for male person; dude
ons	us/we
ons moet die verlede vergeet	we must forget the past
oom	uncle; used by younger people as a respectful term of address for an older male

ou	chap, mate
ouballie	old chap; implying older, 'back in the day' man
ouens	chaps, mates
piel	penis
plek	place
poephol	arsehole
pozzie	position, chosen spot
Rhema	charismatic church
shem	shame
skel	scold; can also be used to mean 'get upset'
smallanyana	little
smiley	sheep's head, roasted or barbecued; a delicacy
soutpiel	literally 'salt penis'; someone with one foot in Africa, one foot in England, with penis in the Atlantic ocean
stem	voice; reference is to the old South African national anthem 'Die Stem'
stirvy	fancy, stuck-up
stoep	veranda
thula	be quiet (instruction)
tik	crystal meth; highly addictive drug
tjommie	friend, mate
tsotsi	bad boy, small-time criminal
ubuntu	fellow feeling of common humanity
umshini wam	bring me my machine gun
voetsek	go, get out of here
vrek	die; usually used in reference to animals
vry	make out
vuvuzela	a horn/trumpet made of plastic; produces single, loud, monotonous note
wus	wimp, coward

Acronyms and abbreviations

AA	Alcoholics Anonymous
ACDP	African Christian Democratic Party
ANC	African National Congress
BEE	black economic empowerment
CEO	chief executive officer
COPE	Congress of the People
COSATU	Congress of South African Trade Unions
DA	Democratic Alliance
EFF	Economic Freedom Fighters
FIFA	Fédération Internationale de Football Association
ID	identity document
ID	Independent Democrats
LGBTI	lesbian, gay, bisexual, transgender, intersex
MP	member of Parliament
PA	personal assistant
PC	politically correct
PE	Port Elizabeth
PR	public relations
RDP	Reconstruction and Development Programme
SAA	South African Airways
SABC	South African Broadcasting Corporation

SAFA	South African Football Association
SRC	Student Representative Council
TRC	Truth and Reconciliation Commission
UCT	University of Cape Town
UWC	University of the Western Cape

PLAY 1
BAFANA REPUBLIC (2007)

Sketch 1

INTERVIEW WITH THE CEO OF THE SOUTH AFRICAN FOOTBALL ASSOCIATION

The actor plays the part of the JOURNALIST *interviewing* HACK, *CEO of SAFA, as well as* HACK *himself. It could be done so that the actor plays the* JOURNALIST *and uses a puppet to represent* HACK, *or so that the voice of the* JOURNALIST *is recorded and the actor plays* HACK *or vice versa.*

JOURNALIST: There's been a lot of controversy about the expenditure on Bafana Bafana's coaches . . . We have the CEO of SAFA (on the line) in the studio. Mr Hack, thank you for (doing this interview) joining us.

HACK: Good morning, Lerato, and good morning to your listeners.

JOURNALIST: Mr Hack, there are rumours that you've imported more coaching staff, not just Mr Perreira . . .

HACK: Yes, Lerato. Thank you for that question. You see, Mr Perreira is the head coach. He gets the boys' minds right. Then we have a bunch of specialist coaches.

JOURNALIST: Like?

HACK: Like a throw-in coach. A free-kick coach. A passing coach. At the end of the day, you can't have just one man doing all these things.

JOURNALIST: Is it true that you also have a left-wing coach?

HACK: Yes, he's from Cuba.

JOURNALIST: And a scoring coach?

HACK: We've hired a Somalian refugee to stand in the goals during practice.

JOURNALIST: Somalia?

HACK: We thought it would help the boys to shoot straight.

JOURNALIST: *And* you have a penalty coach?

HACK: Yes, Lerato. That's how to take them, not how to give them away. In which case, we would have hired a player from the Stormers.

JOURNALIST: That sounds like a lot of coaches.

HACK: And that's not all. We also have a diving coach.

JOURNALIST: A diving coach?

HACK: Lerato, this is a very important part of the modern game, so we've hired someone from Hollywood's Stunts Department to show the boys how to dive in the penalty box.

JOURNALIST: That makes it eight coaches.

HACK: Nine.

JOURNALIST [*bemused*]: Two more and you could make up a whole soccer team of coaches.

HACK: Thanks for that comment, Lerato. Yes, we have our full quota of coaches, but we're still fundraising for one important coach.

JOURNALIST: Which one's that?

HACK: The four-wheeled coach to take the team from the hotel to the stadium.

JOURNALIST: So how *are* you going to get the team to travel?

HACK: Lerato, thank you for that question. We're starting a Bafana Bafana lift scheme. It's called 'Give Bafana a lift, and we'll take you for a ride'.

JOURNALIST: So are you raising funds for the team bus?

HACK: Yes, in fact, straight after this, I'm off to the casino.

JOURNALIST: Oh, so *they're* sponsoring the coach?

HACK: No, we're using some of our sponsors' money as a kind of investment. I've got a poker game. Danny's doing blackjack. And the other SAFA members are playing the slot machines.

JOURNALIST: So you're gambling with the sponsors' money to raise more money?

HACK: Every business has an element of risk, Lerato . . .

JOURNALIST: Just a final question, Mr Hack. Bafana Bafana is ranked 12th in Africa and 60th in the world. No one expects them to get beyond the first round. Isn't all this expenditure on them a waste of money?

HACK [*pauses; reflects*]: The World Cup is not really about *our* soccer team . . .

JOURNALIST: What is it about?

HACK: It's about . . . it's . . . about . . .

JOURNALIST: It's about showcasing Africa . . .

HACK: Exactly! Ja, exactly!

JOURNALIST: Thank you, Mr Hack.

HACK [*imitating* JOURNALIST, *and putting down the receiver*]: 'It's about showcasing Africa . . .' [*Snorts.*] I must remember that one!

Sketch 2

CHARDONNAY

The character is CHARDONNAY, *a footballer's wife. She is chicly dressed. She tells her story through a combination of Alcoholics Anonymous 'confession'-type scenes, with a bottle of wine and a glass to help. She gets progressively drunker, louder and less sophisticated through the course of the scene.*

CHARDONNAY: Hello, my name's Chardonnay. And I'm an alcoholic. [*Takes a sip. Sips again.*] I wasn't always an alcoholic. But then, I haven't always been a footballer's wife. [*Sniggers*]. When I was a cricketer's girlfriend, I was a dagga addict. And when I was engaged to a rugby player, I nearly overdosed on steroids. [*Pours wine into four glasses.*]

I met my husband at a wine tasting. [*Sips from a glass and spits.*] I was there with my friends, Brandy and Savannah. He was very charming. But I should've known. Only weeks after our wedding, he was tasting other wines. There was this white French chick, Chenin. Chenin Blanc. Then there was the red-headed Merle . . . oh . . . different vintage . . . Mature. In fact, bloody old! She could've been his mother.

He even cheated on me with my friends. One day I came home, and he was with Brandy. They were doing coke. Another time he and Savannah had just made out in the pool. Savannah looked at me, all innocent. She was already . . . dry. Once, I found him in bed with Brie, a desperate housewife from around the corner. Unfazed, he asked me to join them. [*Wryly.*] Chardonnay and Brie. I felt like I was at a cheese and wine party.

I suppose I should be grateful. At least he cheats on me with women. My friend, Shiraz . . . her husband was a centre forward. [*Checks to see who's listening, then whispers loudly to audience.*] He came out of the cabernet . . . and now he plays for the other side.

[*This time she takes a swig of wine; takes a chair.*]

Anyway, I decided I would get back at my husband. To see how he liked it if I cheated behind his back. [*Sits on chair, opens and lifts her legs.*] So I did the right back. [*Twists around with the chair's back to audience and as if she's on top of a lover.*] The left back. [*Bends over, facing the audience; looks lustily behind her.*] And the centre back. [*Beat.*] Like they say on the Cape Flats, I became . . . Chardonnaai.

[*Takes a slow sip of wine.*]

My husband's a footballer. He kicks for a living. Sometimes he brings his work home. [*Rubs her stomach and grimaces.*] He could be a goalkeeper. [*Rubs her cheek.*] He has a mean punch. [*Beat.*] At least I'm alive to tell the tale. [*Pours another drink.*] I could've been a policeman's wife, like my sister Cheryl. And I would never know if my children and I would be alive the next day!

[*Drinks a little more, and gets a little more loose-tongued and louder.*]

At least I'm not alone. There's like a whole Footballers Wives' Club. Thank goodness for my support network. I know some women laugh at us . . . [*Sneeringly.*] The Footballers Wives' Club. They think they're superior with their book clubs. Well, we also read! Menus! Labels! [*Quietly.*] Court orders . . . They think all we do is shop and go for facials. But we also do charity work. We raise money for children of single mothers . . . mainly our husbands' illegitimate children.

[*Drinks again.*]

I was pregnant once. I was 14. He was 32. My school teacher. It was a backstreet abortion. I didn't know at the time . . . I would never be able to have kids again. [*Wry smile.*] But that's the year I got my best marks for maths. My mother wanted me to be an accountant. My father still wasn't convinced. He's the one who advised me to snag a rich sportsman. [*Beat.*]

[*Sadly.*] I was lucky. My sister got the policeman. No one else knew. Just me and my teacher. But I felt a twist in my womb every time I was called Chardonnaai.

A child goes missing every six hours in this place. Babies are raped all the time. There are thousands of AIDS orphans. So I can't have children . . . was I cursed or am I blessed?

[*She is now drinking out of the bottle.*]

Anyway, three weeks ago, I'm watching *Days of Our Lives* and the bell rings. It's Mr and Mrs Jansen. And their 15-year-old daughter.

Pink-cheeked Rosé. Full-bodied, but under age. She's pregnant. And she's fingered my husband.

[*Drinks deeply.*]

At first, my husband denies it. Then he admits it. Then he's like . . . she said she was 18. She threw herself at him. She spiked his drink. She rented the hotel room . . . Slut! The girl's mother wants money. The girl's father wants to lay a charge of statutory rape. All the girl wants is to Mxit on her phone.

[*Drinks again.*]

My husband calls me over. He says Mr Jansen's willing to drop the charges if . . . if I sleep with him. My husband says I don't have to do it. What could I do? This is my husband. He's not perfect. But I don't want him to go to jail. I mean, he could get raped.

[*Tries to regain her sophisticated composure.*]

Hello, my name's Chardonnay. And I'm an alcoholic. [*Whispers conspiratorially to the audience.*] But not for long. I'm writing a book. Kiss and tell. It's called 'The Smaller the Dick, the Bigger the Prick'. And I'm launching it in 2010. It will be a best-seller. I'll sell the movie rights. Make a television series. Perhaps I'll get my own talk show. *Tipsy Talk with Chardonnay.* I'll be financially independent. And then I'll be able to walk away . . . free . . . free at last!

Sketch 3

PAHAD REPRESENTATIVE

Lights come up on a chair, stage centre, and PAHAD REPRESENTATIVE *dressed in a raincoat, hat and dark glasses. He is interrogating someone who is seated on the chair.*

PAHAD REPRESENTATIVE: Good evening, Mr Manjatwa. I'm from Patriots Against Heretics and Detractors, PAHAD. [*Beat.*]

No, not PAGAD. PAHAD. We want to know . . . what's your problem? [*Beat.*]

We saw that you wrote a letter to the newspaper yesterday. [*Beat.*]

Did you or did you not write a letter to the newspaper? You did. Exactly. No, no, I don't have to reveal my sources. Do you remember what you wrote? Let me remind you anyway. [*Takes out letter.*]

'Given the challenges of poverty, unemployment, housing, crime, HIV/AIDS, blah, blah, blah, is it the wisest thing to be spending so much money on the 2010 FIFA World Cup?'

[*As he folds up the letter.*] Tell me, are you a racist? [*Beat.*]

Yes, Thomas Manjatwa . . . or is it Uncle Tom? I can see you're black . . . at least on the outside! Tell me something . . . where were you in the struggle for liberation? When we were working our butts off in exile in London, Berlin, Paris so that you could be free, what were you doing? [*Beat.*]

Okay . . . so you were in the United Democratic Front. [*Snorts.*] Everyone was in the United Democratic Front. So tell me . . . did you join the struggle to be poor? [*Beat.*]

Ultra-leftist!

[*Changes tack to 'good cop'.*] I think I know what's going on here. There's a bit of sour grapes . . . you're not getting a bit of the World Cup 'action' . . . am I right? So why don't you start a company? You've got the credentials . . . you're . . . black. You have a bit of a struggle record. [*Beat.*]

Start a construction company . . . everyone's got a construction company. Or shares in one. [*Laughs.*] You don't need to know anything about construction. You're the guy who wins the tender. You take off 25 per cent and then you get the white guys to do the work. [*Beat.*]

It's not illegal . . . it's empowerment, mugu!

Okay, fine. Then don't do it. Disempower yourself! [*Beat. Beat.*]

Tell me something. Who do you work for? The DA? I know they say they want the World Cup, but these honkies don't really care about the beautiful game. They'll do anything to embarrass us, to make a black government look bad . . . even writing letters like this and putting a black name to it!

Okay, so not the DA. Is it Patricia? I know . . . it's the Australians! You're working for the Australians, right? [*Angrily.*] You unpatriotic bastard! You're giving ammunition to our enemies! [*Beat.*]

[*Quietly sinister.*] What do you mean it's your democratic right to ask questions? Who do you think you are? You're not even a deputy minister . . . ! Do you think we'll allow people like you to abuse the freedoms that were bought at a heavy price so that you can undermine our glorious democracy? [*Spits.*] Bloody coconut!

Whinging about crime . . . *real* black people don't whinge about crime, Thomas! It's people like you who have sold out the struggle, Thomas Manjatwa! Once you were with us, but now you're against us, against the people.

But let me tell you something . . . we're watching you. You're on our list . . . of people NOT to invite to the opening of Parliament, or to our special business briefings, to Miss South Africa or to our golf days . . .

As lights fade.

We are watching you . . .

Sketch 4

BHAMJEE

The character is ISSY BHAMJEE, *an Indian entrepreneur. He is flogging goods to customers while making a documentary in which he speaks into the camera.*

BHAMJEE [*into camera*]: So many people have the wrong idea about the Bhamjees, man. Just 'cos my first cousin got caught selling his comps at the World Cup in Germany! Here, you sell your complimentary travel vouchers, you become a mayor! Know what I mean? And just because Roshnie, my third cousin twice removed . . . from Edgars, for shoplifting . . . is also a Bhamjee, doesn't mean we're all the same! I mean, even her own brother, Sershan, prefers Mr Price. People are so quick to stereotype. [*Beat.*] Excuse me, I just have to see to this customer.

Hey, Chetty, I told you not to come in here anymore, man! Okay . . . just this time. What I can do for you? [*Beat.*]

Depends . . . what pirates do you want? We got the latest Pirates of the Caribbean . . . it's not been released yet. We got the latest Orlando Pirates T-shirts and the latest pirate CDs. Just in this morning from my china . . . in India. You can have a look around . . . but Chetty [*warningly*], my security cameras are also having a look around.

[*Into camera.*] So, as I was saying . . . I started this business after seeing a government ad a couple of months ago . . . 'make corruption your business' . . . so I did. You see, now the Bhamjees would be recognised for what we are . . . pioneers! Know what I mean? Long before anyone else was doing it, we were. You know who started Palmalot? My Uncle Srinath. He got rich greasing . . . a lot of palms. That's why it was called Palmalot. Long before this dairy company came along. They only milked cows . . . and their own company. Uncle Srinath fleeced anything that moved.

[*To a customer.*] Yes, sir? [*Beat.*]

Yes, we do have Bafana Bafana stock . . . will that be laughing stock or chicken stock? We also have recycled Bafana condoms . . . only used once. If you're looking for something for your wife, what about the Bafana recipe book? [*Beat.*]

Ja, the book's blank . . . so you can ask the players for their favourite recipes and then you paste them in the book. [*To the camera person.*] Eish, people want everything on a plate nowadays!

[*To interviewer.*] Excuse me . . . [*To customer.*] Yes, ma'am? Yes, we do sell body parts . . . [*laughs*] and it won't cost you an arm and a leg because we get our parts from China. [*Beat.*]

It might be a bit small for you, but yes, they do work, ma'am. We just sold a liver to the health minister . . . now we're waiting to sell her a heart.

We also have a special on children this week . . . but you have to get in quickly before Madonna and Angie come back . . . buy one healthy child and get five AIDS orphans free. [*Beat.*]

Ma'am, if you think that's sick . . . you should've seen their parents. I'm just trying to give these kids a chance . . .

Do you have kids? Then maybe I can interest you in the 2010 magic wand . . . great for vanishing tricks! All you say is 'Abracadabra, FIFA and Blatter', you make a wish like 'Vanish poverty' and, abracadabra, no poverty. But please, ma'am, this is a children's toy . . .

I think government's on the right track . . . sorting out unemployment with this 'make corruption your business' campaign. There's a lot of potential for public-private partnerships. I myself have a few joint ventures with Home Affairs. Like 'one Zimbabwean, two ID books'. [*Beat.*] 'Avoid tax, get a death certificate.'

And I have a half-brother in the Scorpions. The top half. He had his legs amputated after he was shot in the knees by another family . . . but that's another story. He collects evidence, and then I sell it back to the criminals. That's how we help to keep the second economy going.

You see, *we're* doing our bit for the country . . . so before the public paints a stereotype of the Bhamjees, that all Bhamjees are the same . . . let me just say that we prefer to call it . . . franchising.

Lights down, music, cartoons transition.

Sketch 5

KABOUTER BASSON

The character is KABOUTER BASSON, *a scientist, dressed in a white coat and wearing big glasses. He sits behind a table arrayed with vials filled with liquid. He speaks into a Dictaphone.*

BASSON [*into Dictaphone*]: Hello, oom, hello, ouens. It's the 20th of May, and I'm making this tape for you at my office at the Drugs in Sport Testing Institute . . . It's not as grand as my job in the army, but not many places will employ a guy with a name like Kabouter Basson. I've sent in a job application to General De la Rey . . . but there's just been a deathly silence.

But here's the thing, ouens. We might not need De la Rey to take back our country. Serious. This regime is doing a much better job at reducing the black population than we did.

Oom Paul will remember when we killed 69 people at Sharpeville. He always used to say that was his favourite position . . . no, not 69 . . . coming from behind [*laughs*] and shooting. Now they got a public holiday . . . Human Rights Day. Big joke, ouens. Why? Because on every Human Rights Day, 51 people are murdered . . . AND every other day of the year. The good thing, kêrels, is that at least 48 of those 51 . . . are black. Now that's the kind of affirmative action we approve of, nê? [*Laughs.*]

Talking about affirmative action, do you okes want to hear a joke? What do a township and Red Bull have in common? [*Beat.*]

You want a clue? [*Beat.*]

Think Brian Havanna, Aikonah Ndugance, Greyton Paulse . . . What do a township and Red Bull have in common? Ja, they both give you wings! [*Laughs.*]

[*Picks up vial, smells it.*] Johnnie Walker Blue Label. [*Checks label.*] Robert McBride. [*Laughs, cynically.*] He kills a few people and is now head of police. I kill a few people and the only job I can get is testing his piss. [*Angrily.*] That's because my former bosses are spending their time washing people's feet. Blerry hensoppers!

Now they're busy changing street names in your suburb. Ossewabrandwagstraat is now going to be called Robert McBride Avenue. Apparently because he also has a laager mentality . . . Castle Lager. They say they're honouring the heroes who brought them freedom. Freedom? [*Snorts.*] But now you can't walk down the street named after your struggle hero . . . in case you get mugged!

What if they named streets after all the people who were murdered after so-called freedom arrived? Like the Brett Goldin Highway? The Richard Ismail off-ramp. Taliep Petersen Boulevard. Gito Baloi Drive. Dumisani Dlamini Street. Ken Kirsten traffic circle. Jackie Simela Avenue. And these were just some of the country's top artists. They say that artists can now make a living . . . ja, maybe, but the trick is . . . to stay alive. Like John Travolta. [*Sings.*] 'Staying alive . . . staying alive.'

[*He picks up another vial, checks the label.*] Justice Motata. [*Snorts.*] 'I was only drinking tea.' [*Smells the vial; turns up his nose.*] Tea? Tee, hee . . . *Another 50* are killed on the roads *every day* and most of them black too! Crammed like sardines into mobile coffins they call taxis. I'm telling you guys . . . we don't have to do anything . . . black people are killing themselves!

Soon . . . we'll be in the majority! And if you think I've had too much mampoer, that's because you haven't seen the latest AIDS statistics . . . *1 000* vrek every day, almost no whites! [*Beat.*]

There are many people who say that I had something to do with the creation of the HI virus. All *I* want to say is . . . I wish! The drugs I experimented with didn't even come close. The TRC said *we* violated the rights of 22 000. This *regime* just lets 362 000 people die every year . . . and these are people who vote for them! And they called *me* Dr Death! They said *we* were racist! But now you know why there's a need for land reform, oom . . . they need the land to bury the dead!

Just a few more years, ouens . . . then we can take back our country. The three million white people will be in the majority! We must remember to honour those who helped us in *our* struggle. We must create a monument to the minister of safety and security . . . and to the minister of transport. But mostly, we must honour Mbeki and Manto . . . it doesn't have to be an airport, or even a street. Maybe just a garlic patch . . . we'll call it the Manto. And in honour of the African Renaissance that buried more people than us racist bastards . . . the African Pathabo.

Lights fade to black, transition to the next sketch, cartoon and chorus of the song 'De la Rey' plays.

Sketch 6

BAFANA IDOLS

In this sketch, there is interplay between the screen with different Idols JUDGES *making comments (recorded) and the actor, who plays the roles of four different contestants. Alternatively, the voices are recorded and projected from within the audience. While the* JUDGES *make comments on the performance, the actor changes into the costume of the next singer, with each costume being sufficient to suggest the character. On screen is a big sign: Bafana Idols Competition.*

JUDGE 1 [*on screen*]: Welcome to *Bafana Idols*. What's your name?

Lights come up on JACKIE VOOMA *dressed in traditional Zulu garb.*

JACKIE: Jackie Vooma.

JUDGE 1: Okay, Jackie. As you know, the winner of this competition will sing at the opening of the World Cup in 2010. The losers will have a choice of watching all the Bafana games or a video of the Proteas World Cup semi-final. So what are you going to sing?

JACKIE: 'Bring Me My Washing Machine'.

[*To the tune of Zuma's 'Umshini wami' ('Bring me my machine gun').*]

She is . . . a young woman
I am . . . a Zulu man
She definitely wants me
I must do what I can
Father of the nation
Premature ejaculation
Oh dear, the sheet's a mess
There is no time to rest
Bring my washing machine
To make the sheets clean
Before my wives get here
And smell something queer

JUDGE 2: No, it doesn't work for me.
JUDGE 3: Too culturally specific.

JUDGE 1: Sorry, Jackie, it's a no.

JACKIE *storms out.* MABEL *enters in Kaapse Klopse costume.*

JUDGE 3: Hello, Mabel. Welcome to *Bafana Idols*. You know the drill. Please go ahead.

MABEL [*to the tune of 'Daar Kom Die Alabama'*]:

> Daar kom al die bafana
> In hul mercs, en hul benz en ook van oorsee
> Daar kom al die bafana
> Virrie land en die mense te kom speel
>
> Maar waar is Bennie? En waar is Quinton?
> Hulle maak hul fortunes in Londen
> Hulle sonde, hul's lief vir ponde
> En hou nie van die land se rand
> As hul terugkom, sal hulle SAFA
> Willie speel nie, nee, nie vir Bafana
> Nou sê die coach, hy's nie getik
> Want sy pay-check is lekker dik
>
> Daar kom al die bafana
> In hul mercs, en hul benz maar nie van oorsee
> Daar kom al die bafana
> Vir jou vrou en jou dogters te kom steel

JUDGE 2: What language is that?

JUDGE 1: I don't think it's national enough.

JUDGE 3: Ja, too Kaaps. Not black enough. Sorry, Mabel.

The lights come up on MANUAL *singing the third* Idols *song.*

JUDGE 2: And you are?

MANUAL: Manual.

JUDGE 3: Manual?

MANUAL: Manual Gear.

JUDGE 1: Okay, Manual. Take it away.

MANUAL [*to the tune of the American national anthem*]:

O say can't you see by the Renaissance light
The FIFA World Cup is what we've all been dreaming
If we keep this thing tight and we play our cards right
It should make a few rich and deliver Mercs gleaming
This is Africa's cup, so we might even share
With our brothers and sisters [*points far away*] who die over there
O South Africa, America of Africa
The land of BEE and the home of the grave.

JUDGE 1: Too much of a cover version.
JUDGE 2: He hit the right notes, but it's not for us.
JUDGE 3: Sorry, Manual, it's a no.

Lights come up on MARLIZE *wearing a Boer outfit.*

JUDGE 2: Okay, meisie, so what are you going to sing for us?
MARLIZE: 'Van der Spuy'.

[*To the tune of the song 'De la Rey'.*]

Op 'n bed in die nag
Lê ons in donker en . . . wag
Ek's 'n moeder met kind en geen hoop
Geen werk, net 'n lyf te verkoop
In my huis is ek baas
Maar geen brood of kaas
Dis van honger ek ly
En die honger en dors
Brand nou diep, diep binne my

Van der Spuy, Van der Spuy
Sal jy ons hoere kom vry want ons ly, Van der Spuy
Ons is kaal, kom betaal
Dan mag ons eet nog een maal, asseblief, Van der Spuy

En die khakis wat wag
Julle's ook welkom
Op my matras
Maar die boer is nog diep en ons rus

Dis nog nie verby
Want die wors van 'n boer
Is dieper en wyer
Jul moet dit sien
Soos 'n perd kom hy in
Die leeu loop van Wes Transvaal

Van der Spuy, Van der Spuy
Sal jy ons hoere kom vry want ons ly, Van der Spuy
Ons is kaal, kom betaal
Dan mag ons eet nog een maal, asseblief, Van der Spuy

[MARLIZE *gets crowd to join her in singing the chorus. She takes out a lighter, raises it in the air, lights it and sings.*]

Lights fade.

PLAY 2
BAFANA REPUBLIC: EXTRA TIME (2008)

Sketch 1

WORLD CUP AMBASSADOR, HAYI BUTI

The character is HAYI BUTI, *an ambassador for the 2010 World Cup to be staged in South Africa. Actor wears a Madiba shirt.*

HAYI BUTI [*in upbeat, gung-ho tone*]: Ladies and gentlemen, thank you for inviting me to address this prestigious dinner in my capacity as the ambassador for the first Football World Cup to be held in Africa. My name is Hayi Buti and I was appointed to my present job by the current president of Mbekistan. For those of you not familiar with African geography, Mbekistan is a breakaway homeland in South Africa, just south of Polokwane. The national diet is humble pie and beetroot, and it gets its water from the deep river of De Nial.

Before taking up this post, I served as a quiet diplomat in Zimbabwe. Maybe that's why you haven't heard of me? I'm proud to say that because of our efforts, we've been able to make the Zimbabwe Ruins accessible across the whole country.

My job in Europe is to put to rest any doubting Thomases, Dickses and Harryses who are unsure about Africa's ability to host the Cup. There are some who still think of Africa as the dark continent. And I know this perception is reinforced by Eskom. But on behalf of our beloved president, I would like to share a poem by a famous African poet, William Bleke:

> Asian Tiger burning bright
> We envy you in our candlelight
> But on we go to 2010
> We hope to have some light by then.

You will notice that I speak of the African World Cup. Not the 2010 World Cup. Nor the 2012 World Cup. Not even the 2015 World Cup. For we refuse to be bulldozed by colonial notions of 'time'.

What I would like to say to any doubters out there is simple: look at our record. Our country has already won a 2010 World Cup. [*Proudly.*] It was last year in France that our Springboks won the Rugby World Cup, on the 20th of October, the 20th of the tenth month. You have your 9/11. We have our 20/10.

Lights fade. The screen explodes into life with some stunning football skills and goals by African soccer players. It plays against the background of a funky soundtrack of African music.

After 35–45 seconds, the lights come up, the screen images fade.

Sketch 2

REALITY SHOW MEDLEY

The character is the PRESENTER/HOST *for each of four well-known, long-running TV reality shows.*

FX: Music. Voice: 'And now, ladies and gentlemen, the South African reality show medley!'

Actor enters.

Music to introduce reality show Survivor.

PRESENTER: Welcome to another edition of *Survivor*, this time played in the wild jungle of South African sport! With dangers lurking after every board meeting!

On my left, we have a motley tribe made up of coaches! Most of the tribe have been voted out, but these coaches have already survived a whole week in their jobs! Let's see if they will win indemnity for another week!

On my right, we have a tribe of players: 5 blacks, 1 coloured, 1 Indian of Muslim descent, one half-Afrikaans white and a disabled lesbian Jew.

Tribes ready? For today's challenge . . . you have to win the World Cup. [*Beat.*] That's it! *Any* World Cup.

[*Listens.*] Er, no. If you win the World Cup, it doesn't mean you'll win immunity. The only way to get immunity is to become . . .

Drum roll.

A sports administrator!

Survivors ready?

Lights half-fade. Music to introduce the reality show The Biggest Loser.

PRESENTER: We have four contestants in this week's Biggest Loser competition!

Weighing in at 240 kilograms is Mr Tshabalala, member of the executive of the South African Football Association. He once played soccer for his school team, but was kicked out when he ate all the doughnuts during half-time. Mr Tshabalala has now gone on to higher things, scoring lots of kilograms with his First Class lifestyle. He even manages to attend a few games when the catering is sponsored.

Then, at 264 kilograms, is Mr Pienaar from the South African Rugby Football Association. He has been working on his build from the days of rugby, braaivleis, sunny skies and Chevrolet and is always to be seen in the scrum for food!

Then, weighing in at a sprightly 218 kilos, is Mr Petersen, vice chairperson of – or maybe it's chairperson of vice – Cricket South Africa. He no longer tours Pakistan because of his drinking problem. His administration skills are suspect, but he knows a good coconut when he sees one.

Finally, we have Mrs Khumalo from the parliamentary committee on sport, who lost a few kilos while monitoring the election in Zimbabwe but still comes in at a whopping 302 kilos. She couldn't help them count the votes, but neither can she count calories. Her favourite dish is blackened wings!

These are some of the administrators and politicians responsible for sport in our country. And all because of interfering incompetents like these, the biggest losers are . . . YOU! The fans!

Lights half-fade. Music to introduce the reality show The Weakest Link.

PRESENTER: Who hired Carlos Perreira at R1.8 million a month and forgot to give him homesick pills?

Who declined to negotiate a new contract with Jake White because he did not transform his surname?

Who pays themselves huge bonuses for having one of the worst football teams on the continent?

Who put themselves in Business Class while disabled athletes sat in Economy Class because they – apparently – didn't need the legroom?

The answer I'm looking for is . . . 'sports administrators'. Sports administrators are the Weakest Link. Goodbye!'

Lights half-fade. Music to introduce the reality show The Amazing Race.

PRESENTER: And in this edition of *The Amazing Race,* we have ten stadiums competing to make the 2010 deadline. [*Adopts horse-racing commentary tone.*] And they're off! It's Soccer City in the lead, followed by Mbombela in Mpumalanga, then Polokwane's Peter Mokaba followed by Royal Bafokeng, with Green Point bringing up the rear.

[*Continuing in horse-race commentary mode.*] Now there are a few delays. It's raining in Cape Town. They're striking in Joburg and a middleman is demanding his cut in Mpumalanga. It's Vodacom Park in the lead, Loftus not far behind and Soccer City has fallen back, with Green Point bringing up the rear.

They've run out of materials in PE. Cranes have broken down in Mmabatho and there's a court case in Cape Town, with Green Point bringing up the rear.

Now it's rolling blackouts in the north, load-shedding in the east, electricity-saving in the west and politicians are fighting in the Cape, and it's Green Point Stadium bringing up the rear . . .

[*As race announcer.*] Green Point Stadium, you are the last to arrive. But since it's you that FIFA wants, we'll eliminate . . . the Athlone Stadium.

Lights fade. Images of Africa and the Big Five.

Sketch 3

AMERICAN AND FRENCHIE ON SAFARI

This sketch has two distinct characters represented by puppets: an American investor and a French talent scout looking for African soccer talent. They are on an African safari together.

AMERICAN [*reciting as in a military workout*]:
> You don't know what I've been told!
> Biofuel is the next gold!

FRENCHIE: Shh . . . ! You'll scare off the game!

AMERICAN: Ah, that's okay. I don't like cricket!

FRENCHIE [*irritated*]: Not cricket! Elephants! Lions!

AMERICAN: Oh . . . where?

FRENCHIE: Here!

AMERICAN: What's this?

FRENCHIE: Hunting for Beginners . . .

AMERICAN: How long have you been doing this?

FRENCHIE: Centuries.

AMERICAN: Really?

FRENCHIE: Why do you think a third of our football team comes from Africa?

AMERICAN: Like 90 per cent of our basketball teams.

FRENCHIE: See? Slavery wasn't all bad!

[*They laugh.*]

AMERICAN: But now we can let them slave away right here! We don't have to bring them with all their children and diseases to our countries anymore! And we can pay them 50 times less than the going rate at home!

FRENCHIE [*laughs*]: Slavery! What were we thinking!

[*They both laugh.*]

FRENCHIE: And when you *do* need someone skilled, you can come here and hunt for the best. Nurses. Teachers. Even musicians.

AMERICAN: What are *you* hunting?

FRENCHIE: African footballers for Europe.

AMERICAN: How's it going?

FRENCHIE: Well, so far I've got an indomitable lion from Cameroon, two super eagles from Nigeria, a couple of elephants from the Ivory Coast and a desert fox from Algeria.

AMERICAN: Not bad!

FRENCHIE: And what are *you* doing here?

AMERICAN: I love the bush.

FRENCHIE [*under his breath to audience*]: Of course, he's American . . . ! He loves Bush!

AMERICAN: And I've come to buy a football team . . .

FRENCHIE: A whole team?

AMERICAN: All my friends are doing it . . . Manchester United. Liverpool.

FRENCHIE [*in a nudge, nudge, wink, wink kind of way*]: But it's cheaper in Africa . . .

AMERICAN: Bloody bargains!

FRENCHIE: Where are you thinking of buying?

AMERICAN: South Africa. They have a team . . . Banana Banana or something . . . like your typical African republic . . . bunch of losers.

FRENCHIE: They're selling their team?

AMERICA: Practically giving it away . . . But that's just for my tax write-off. I'm actually in maize.

FRENCHIE: Maize? You grow food?

AMERICAN: That's all you Frogs think of . . . food. I'm talking biofuel. Have you seen how much land is out there? And the labour's cheap!

FRENCHIE: I know. We pay these footballers for a week what 10 000 workers here make in a year! And then they want the footballer to come back and play for his country . . . for peanuts!

AMERICAN: Bloody monkeys!

[FRENCHIE *doesn't respond.*]

AMERICAN: Peanuts . . . monkeys . . . get it?

FRENCHIE: That's not funny. I deplore racism!

AMERICAN: Hey, me too, me too. I voted for Obama . . .

FRENCHIE: Shh!

AMERICAN [*whispers*]: What?

FRENCHIE: A black antelope . . . Angolan!

A shot rings out.

AMERICAN: Damn! You're good!

FRENCHIE: I know . . . I'm French!

AMERICAN: But we're still better than you . . .

FRENCHIE: Impossible . . . !

AMERICAN: We've got ourselves a black president!

FRENCHIE: Just one? We've bought black presidents all over Africa . . . !

Lights fade.

Sketch 4

AA ON-SCREEN FILLERS

There are three AA on-screen fillers for the director to use at appropriate times. They can either be filmed and used as links between sketches, or they can be performed by the actor, or both.

AA is the acronym for Alcoholics Anonymous, but here it is used for a variety of similar therapy sessions. In the background of each sketch is an AA sign. It becomes clear during the sketch what the AA in each sketch refers to.

The character in the first on-screen filler is FANIE; *in the second it is* JABU; *in the third it is* BOKKIE.

The actor is wearing a scrum cap.

FANIE: Hello, my name is Fanie van Schalkwyk – no relation to Marthinus [*spits*] – and I'm a victim of affirmative action.

GENERAL: *Hello, Fanie . . .*

FANIE: Where I come from, it's every boy's dream to play for the Springboks. That [*smiles goofily*] and to marry Charlize Theron. But I don't have the height of a lock. I'm too light for the front row. And now . . . I'm too white for a wing.

My father – Piston – used to play for the Bokke. He tells me it was almost impossible for a soutpiel to get into the national rugby team, let alone a person of colour.

But why should I pay for the sins of my father's generation? I was three years old when Mr Madiba was released from prison. We're all equal now. Hey? But like my dad says, the whole world is going blackwards. Lewis Hamilton is Formula One champion. Usain Bolt is the fastest man in the world. Obama is president of the United States. And it was coloureds – the Chinese – who cleaned up at the Olympic Games.

So I'm emigrating to New Zealand. I'm still young. Their team is called the All Blacks, but at least they still have space for whites.

Music, fade.

JABU: Hello, my name is Jabu Molebatsi, and I'm an alcoholic.

GENERAL: *Hello, Jabu . . .*

JABU: Hello, Ricky Januarie. Hello, Herschelle. We even have some internationals here. Jimmy Cowan. The two Andrews: Symonds and Flintoff. We're obviously in the wrong job, guys. If Ricky was a judge, he'd be taking up court time to save his career. Herschelle, if you were a police chief like McBride, you'd be given a promotion. And if I was Tony Yengeni, I'd be on my way to becoming a minister!

But I'm not bitter. I admit I have a problem. The coach first noticed it when I kept vomiting on the Bafana Bafana jersey. And that was before they told us that we were ranked 85th in the world!

Many people have asked how the richest country on the continent has sixteen African teams ranked above it. The simple answer is they score more. We don't score. Well, not on the pitch. [*Smiles goofily.*]

I know that as sports stars, we have a responsibility as role models, especially for the youth. That is why I am here today, to clean up my act, so that Bafana's results will be a better inspiration for young people than Julius Malema's matric results.

Lights fade.

The actor is an animal; it looks really nervous.

BOKKIE: Hello, my name is Bokkie, and I'm on the endangered species list.

GENERAL: *Hello, Bokkie . . .*

BOKKIE: I've won two World Cups. Lost my stem. Learned to sing 'God Bless Africa'. In Sotho! Got a black majority backline. And now even a black front row!

I've outflanked the lions. Outwitted the cockerels. Outmuscled the wallabies. But outraged the cannibals. And they're not all black. Luke. There's Cheeky. I feel nauseous. Have to run. Just to say, there's hope. Maybe I'll survive. Living in the shadow of the King Protea! [*Vomits exaggeratedly.*]

Sketch 5

A MAN'S GAME

The character is a 13-year-old CHILD SOLDIER. *He wears a headband and carries a revolver behind his back, which he pulls out later in the monologue.*

CHILD SOLDIER: Where were you when they said 'the World Cup's going to Africa'? My father was listening to the radio. My mother was selling vegetables at our stall in the village. School was over. I was outside. Playing football with my friends.

[*Like a sports commentator.*] 'Gwandoya passes to Kigongo. Kigongo up the middle. He sends a through ball to Akiki [*getting more excited*], who crosses to Lutalo' [*to audience*] – that's me. 'Lutalo traps the ball. He dribbles past one defender. Goes round another. Lutalo shoots! [*Raises his arms triumphantly.*] Gooooaaalllll!'

My father runs out excited. 'We got it, Lutalo! We got it!' Got what? 'The World Cup! It's coming to Africa!'

He was excited. A lot more excited than when George Bush came to Africa. The World Cup's like our saviour! We started singing 'The World Cup's coming to Africa! The World Cup's coming to Africa!'

'We must start saving,' my father interrupted. 'We've got a few years. I'm taking you to South Africa in 2010.' [*Big-eyed, as son.*] South Africa? Will I see Mandela? [*As father.*] 'Maybe. You'll nearly be finished with high school. We can look for a place for you to study there.' [*Disappointed, as son.*] Study? [*As father.*] 'You can't just play football, Lutalo! You must study to get a good job.'

[*Reflecting, childlike.*] I wonder if Drogba's father ever told *him* that . . .

We were about to restart our game. Then we heard the whistles. But we didn't have a referee. Where was the whistling from? First from that way. Then behind us. Then from there. Then all around us. Then there were the shots. And only then we saw them. About 20 . . . 25 of them. Closing in. Surrounding the pitch. Pointing their guns at us. This wasn't supposed to happen here. Our village was safe. There were government soldiers here. But it *was* happening. Our parents' worst nightmare.

Akiki tried to run away. They caught him. And then they . . . shot him. In the head. One minute he was a centre forward. The next minute he was on his back, dead. They said nothing. Their guns said everything. They took 13 of us that day . . . My father, on his knees, an AK pointed at him, helpless.

I try not to remember. Memories like that make me weak. They make me sad. Like a child. But I'm not a child! I'm a man! A soldier! Fighting for the freedom of my people!

I still play soccer in our spare time. But not with many of the friends from my village. Gwandoya had his legs blown off by a landmine. Now we call him 'Footloose'. [*Laughs.*] Kigongo tried to escape and was shot. Traitor! Magomu . . . poor Magomu . . . he messed with the commander's girlfriend and had his dick chopped off. [*Laughs hysterically.*] But that was after the commander shot his girlfriend. And forced Magomu to have sex with the body. In front of all of us. [*Wry smile.*] The commander says Magomu can't score anymore . . .

Last night, we watched television. Brazil against Chile. We were all Brazilians. 'Shoot! Shoot! Shoot!' we all shouted whenever the strikers had the ball! [*Beat.*] [*Remembers; tone changes.*] It was like my first time. We were just outside our camp. There was a man tied to a tree. The commander said he was a spy. He gave me a gun. [*Pulls out the revolver from behind his back.*] All around me, they began to chant 'Shoot! Shoot! Shoot!' I missed. The commander made me go closer. [*He moves towards the audience.*] I hit the man in the shoulder. Closer. [*Gets as close to the audience as possible.*] I couldn't miss. [*Elated.*] Yes! I scored!

It got easier and easier. We used to go to a place. Line everyone up. Get them to raise their hands in the air. Then shoot from the one side to the centre, and then from the other side to the centre. We called it the Mexican Wave. [*Laughs hysterically.*] The commander gave me a trophy. Leading striker! Thirty-seven goals in one week!

I wish my parents could see me! They would be proud of the name they gave me. Lutalo! Fighter! Warrior!

The commander says the way things are going, we'll soon have our freedom! I ask him if it will be before the World Cup in 2010. 'Why?' he laughs. 'Even then you'll be too young to make the national team. Soccer's a man's game.'

Lights fade.

Sketch 6

ABC TAKE-OUT

Through a parody of the alphabet song, this sketch comments on the burden on taxpayers to pay for the costs of hosting the 2010 FIFA World Cup.

On screen: 'And now for a word from our sponsors'. In the red and yellow colours of McDonald's: 'McDonald's, proud sponsor of the 2010 World Cup, supports literacy in Africa. Every child should be able to read and say "SUPERSIZE!"'

[*As* CHILD *reciting the alphabet as at primary school*]:

A is for Africa
Virgin Cup hosts
B's for Bafana
Who can't find the posts

C is for Coach
Brought in from abroad
Paid in D-Dollars
So at least, *he* scored!

E is for Egypt
Africa's champs
F is for Floodlights . . .
And G . . . for Gas lamps

H for Home game
At least we'll have three
To I for Insult
Add Injury

J's for June's start
In a few hundred days
But K'll be for Kak-off
Caused by delays

L's for Laduma
We shout when we score

Oh please, please Bafana
Let us shout once More!

N is for Nando's
With left and right wings
O is for Offside
That rhymes with . . . nothing

P's for Police
That thin, thin blue line
At least during the Cup
We should be fine

Q? Qualifiers . . .
Which we don't have to play
'Cos we're in the World Cup
We just had to pay

R is for Ranking
We're 69 . . .
S is for Stadiums
Two billion a time

T is for Third Force
We'll give them the blame
Not for our Ups
But for losing each game

V? Vuvuzela!
W? Whistleblower!
X? Xenophobia
Z? Zuma's shower!

And Y is for You
Eternal taxpayer

For the A.B.C.
Of the F.I.F.A.
Is for the next 40 years
You'll have to pay!

Sketch 7

SECURITY CHIEF

The character is someone who revels in security, a former senior officer in the old South African Defence Force, a man who loves being in charge. He has only one arm and he is dressed in a security-type jacket. His accent is old Afrikaans, grammatically clumsy. At one level, the sketch is about prejudice towards the 'other', people who 'wear towels'. At another level, it is about an old soldier, rejected by the new South Africa, now feeling wanted again. Once castrated, now being restored to manhood.

SECURITY CHIEF: Manne! Welcome back from Iraq! I hope you made lots of dollars, and that it made up for your nearly having your heads chopped off on the 8 o'clock news! [*Laughs.*]

Now, ordinarily, many of you can't be employed in terms of our country's employment equity laws, because you are the wrong colour. Which is why you were given packages to leave the Defence Force in the first place. But I am able to employ up to 2 per cent disabled persons. So, the war in Iraq might have cost you an arm or a leg, but say hello to security work in the new South Africa as an affirmative action employee! Those of you who can still do it, give the guy next to you a high five! Yes!

Manne, it's like old times! Like you, I don't care much for soccer. It's a game for girls. But if nothing else, the FIFA World Cup will give us the chance to be men again! Security men!

So listen up! We're in the midst of a new total onslaught. And it's moerse exciting! Don't take it from me, take it from George W Bush. The threat, gentlemen, is coming from ouens running around with towels around their heads!

A picture of Osama bin Laden comes up on screen.

You all know about 9/11. [*Conspiratorially.*] Intelligence has come up with an interesting theory. Nine and 11 make 20. And the number missing between 9 and 11 is 10. The good money says that the next big total onslaught by the towel-heads will be 2010!

[*Loudly again.*] You have been recruited because of your expertise. The task of this unit are to secure the skies and related areas. To do whatever it takes.

So, gentlemen, here are our 2010 ten-point plan:

One: We spread disinformation. We let the towel-heads think that the World Cup are in Australia. Let them bomb Australia. Some of you may have heard rumours about the World Cup moving to Australia. [*Winks.*] That are part of our disinformation strategy.

Two: Only pork are to be served on all incoming flights to South Africa for one month before, and during, the World Cup, to discourage towel-heads from flying here.

Three: The only movie to be shown on incoming flights during that time will be *The Passion of the Christ,* to further root out any towel-heads intent on attacking our civilisation and way of life.

Four: All teams will be required to change on the pitch in full view of spectators, to ensure that no one are wearing a suicide vest.

Five: If you can't take it on the plane, you can't take it to the game! That rule means no dangerous weapons like water, perfume, hair gel, cooldrink and toothpaste will be allowed into the stadiums.

Six: Men's toilets are the favourite place for cells to meet before carrying out their evil plans. Accordingly, it will be illegal for men to go to the toilet during the World Cup.

Seven: Football stadiums are now national security areas. Anyone caught filming or photographing a stadium will be detained and renditioned to Guata . . . Gatsha . . . Guada . . . that place! until after the World Cup.

Eight: All stadiums will be declared no-fly zones. And I mean, no fly! There will be no aeroplanes, helicopters, microlight aircraft, remote-control children's planes, kites, birds . . . Even a mozzie – by that I mean mosquito – will not be allowed in!

Nine: . . . fok, there is no nine. And there's no eleven. So, moving along.

Ten: Home Affairs will issue a special identity document for everyone who has a valid ticket to a game. No ID, no entry. Home Affairs? [*Snorts.*] The stadiums are going to be empty, ouens, but they will be safe!

[*Hands behind his back, feet astride.*] For some this are a game. For us, this are a war. Gentlemen, the war on terror are coming to our country! Bring it on! Our country needs us again!

At ease! That's all for this week. Next week's workshop [*checks his paper*], it says here . . . will be on cultural diversity training. Ja, whatever!

Screen fades.

Sketch 8

BAFANA ELECTION FEVER

The actor sits on a chair with headphones. On his right hand is a woman puppet – PRESENTER – covering his whole hand. On his left hand are five finger puppets, each representing a different political party. Each puppet is in the colours of the respective party.

Music.

PRESENTER [*over-the-top Model C accent*]: This is Radio 702. With the elections in 2009 and the World Cup in 2010, we've asked today's roundtable of political parties to tell us what they will do to help Bafana Bafana if they came to power.

We'll start with the ruling party. Please tell us what the ANC stands for.

ANC FINGER PUPPET [middle finger] [*earnest, boring, monotone*]: Dogs, snakes and other counter-revolutionaries say that A.N.C. stands for Arrogance. Nepotism. Corruption. But these are the initials of our movement's true icons: A for Albert Luthuli. N for Nelson Mandela. And C for . . . for Comrade Zuma.

Thank you for this opportunity to speak to the public, especially since *our* public broadcaster was hijacked by Mbeki's tsotsis.

Why should you join our party? First, we'll keep you young. You can play in our youth league till you're 40. And with life expectancy now at 49, with us, you can stay young till you die! All this is possible since we replaced the RDP with the RIP.

But there are other reasons to join us. If you're one of our MPs and you defraud Parliament, we'll shift the goalposts. When the opposition forces us into a corner, we'll give them the race card. And when our members are sent to jail, we'll get them out early. We call that . . . half-time.

PRESENTER: That's all very well, but what are you going to do about Bafana Bafana?

ANC FINGER PUPPET [*incredulously*]: Nothing. [*Beat.*] The national football team is *already* transformed.

PRESENTER: Okay, thank you. Now I'd like the African Christian Democratic Party to make their pitch. And please try to stick to the point about Bafana.

ACDP FINGER PUPPET [pinky] [*speaks like a preacher*]: We have a four-point plan to turn Bafana Bafana into a winning team.

First, we would ensure that every member of the squad is married. We don't believe in scoring before marriage.

Second, we will ban hugging after a goal is scored. This only encourages the abomination of homosexuality.

Thirdly, there are obvious divisions in the team. The left wing doesn't know what the right wing is doing. You can't send out a team on a wing and a prayer. So we would ensure that Bafana sings from the same hymn book.

And finally, the one thing that we all miss – just like Bafana in front of the posts – is the penalty. To turn us into a winning nation again, we would bring back the penalty. The death penalty!

Hallelujah!

PRESENTER: Thank you, Reverend. And now for the new kids on the block, the Congress of the People . . . or whatever their name is today.

COPE FINGER PUPPER [thumb] [*speaks fast, in a used-car salesman kind of way*]: Everyone wants to know how the Congress of the People differs from the ANC. First, they may have Julius Malema, [*proudly*] but we have Peter Marais! The real difference though – to use a soccer analogy – is that we are professionals. They are amateurs.

Take their slogan that they will kill for Zuma. Well, we already killed for Mbeki! [*Proudly.*] More than 300 000 people died of AIDS while we were loyal to the president. [*Sniggers.*] Now there are 300 000 fewer votes for the ANC!

Then take their favourite karaoke song . . . These amateurs sing about bringing their machine guns. [*Dismissive snigger.*] [*Smugly.*] During our time in government we bought submarines! Corvettes! Helicopters! Fighter jets!

And do I have to remind you of the records that we achieved? Record unemployment! The biggest gap between rich and poor! The highest number of people infected with HIV . . . in the world!

And it was during *our* time that Bafana fell 40 places in the world rankings!

So vote COPE! Help us to cut the power of the ANC! Remember, it is us who have the experience in bringing you power cuts!

PRESENTER: Thank you, COPE. And now it's the turn of the Independent Democrats.

ID FINGER PUPPET [ring finger] [*conspiratorially*]: The ID has received a secret dossier claiming that Bafana Bafana is throwing games deliberately. For a long time we have suspected that there is corruption in football. There is no way that we can have the best strikers in COSATU, and yet Bafana Bafana can't score goals.

We demand a judicial inquiry to investigate if the devil is making Bafana lose games in exchange for bribes! We want Judge Heath to be part of this investigation.

We call on anyone – like referees and other whistle-blowers – to come forward with information. It's time to take the kickback out of local soccer, so that we can kick butt again!

PRESENTER: Thank you. Patricia. And now for the Democratic Alliance.

DA FINGER PUPPET [index finger] [*tough, aggressive*]: If the Democratic Alliance knows anything, then it's how to be a tough opposition! Vote for us, and we'll toughen up Bafana Bafana. First, we'll appoint a white as coach. Jake White. He's won a World Cup, so he should be able to help Bafana beat . . . Lesotho!

Second, we'll demand that the demographics of the national team be transformed. At the very least, we would like to see two white wings.

Thirdly, we believe that Bafana needs a symbol they can believe in, something they can play for and be proud of. So, we will move the springbok to the Bafana Bafana jersey – right in between the protea and the white flag. Our critics accuse us of defending white privilege. They say we attack the ruling party on every front. We promise to make that our game plan for Bafana Bafana. Attack will be our best form of defence. Vote DA for a national team that will get into the World Cup on merit! And not because we pay R20 billion for them to enter!

PRESENTER: That's all we have time for this week. Tune in again next week for another hot-air discussion on . . . global warming.

Sketch 9

VUVUZELA SALESMAN

The character represents a PRESENTER *on a television shopping channel.*

PRESENTER: Don't delay. Phone now. Unused stadiums. Going cheaply. Call 2010-2010-2010.

If you buy a stadium [*takes out a vuvuzela*], you get this piece of plastic – absolutely free!

But that's not all!

Phone now, and you will get full operating instructions. In 11 official languages. And Braille. Especially for referees.

[*Holding up the vuvuzela.*] Support democracy in Africa. One-man-one-note. [*Blows vuvuzela.*]

The vuvuzela! Mating call of an elephant! So, use it at a game, not at a game park! Not to be confused with the vukazuma, the call of our president-in-mating!

With this piece of plastic, you can . . . make a noise!

But that's not all!

For a few rand more, we can fit it with a telescopic lens, so you can watch the game even from the cheap seats. [*Holds vuvuzela to eye as if it's a telescope.*]

Or use it for breathalyser tests. Next time, see how much alcohol your favourite politician has consumed by testing how much noise they can make. [*Drunkenly, tries to blow, and no sound comes out.*]

But even that's not all!

Vuvuzelas make wonderful candlesticks! With every vuvuzela, we will give you a free candle! For those night games. Just in case!

Picture of upside-down vuvuzelas with candles burning at the blow end.

Keep it in your car! If your hooter packs up, blow your own horn! Or use it to pour petrol into your tank . . .

Lights fade. Footage of fans blowing vuvuzelas.

Sketch 10

WHINGE

This sketch is played as a stand-up comic. The actor is to play this with a fast, sharp energy, acting out as much of the story as possible. He enters, running, smiling, as a rapper.

Yo yo
I'm a boy from the 'hood
And I made good
Playing the game
Winning fame
It's not the same
For my homies
Who stayed
Who prayed
For things to get better
I played
And things *are* better

I packed up my bags
For a foreign clime
Took off my talent
To earn me a dime
Now I drink in euros
And dress to the nines
I party in dollars
Pull babes all the time

When I go back home
Buy my homies a drink
When I go back home
Next time I think
I'll buy my country
Yo, peace y'all!

Thank you! Thank you! Wow! What a great audience! That's my tribute to Benni McCarthy . . . Arsehole!

Sketch 11

STAND-UP COMIC

This sketch is played as a stand-up comic.

So I'm going to end off tonight's show and tell you about my recent trip. I was checking in at Cape Town International, and right behind me were Mr and Mrs Whinge and their 17-year-old daughter, Whingey. It was a typical queue: 65% tourists with their wooden giraffes; 10% government officials on yet another fact-finding mission; 10% business people to help government officials interpret the facts; and 15% Whinge families, packing for Perth or leaving for London. Certainly not hurrying to Harare. The long queue moved slowly, which had Mr and Mrs Whinge sniggering, 'And *they* want to host the World Cup!' It didn't strike them that it was a BA flight. With BA staff. Last time I checked, BA wasn't hosting the World Cup!

We arrive in London, 30 minutes early. But, we're *too* early. There's still a plane parked in our berth. So we sit in the plane. On the tarmac. An hour after landing, we get off the plane. I smile at Mr Whinge, 'And these people want to host the Olympics . . .'

I make my way towards the KLM check-in counter. We board the plane and we arrive at Schiphol. I don't notice there are two queues, one for EU passport holders and another for terrorist suspects. I stand in the shorter EU queue. The little official with pimples the size of his ego looks at my passport, and then says – loudly – 'Can't you read?' He points to the sign . . . Friendly place this. Especially for people like me who wouldn't get the lead role in Snow White . . .

I wait at the baggage conveyor belt. And wait. Everyone's got their bags. Except me. I go to the baggage Help Desk. The 'Help Desk' proceeds to interrogate me like I'm the head of al-Qaeda: 'Are you sure you checked it in?' 'What did it look like?' 'Where are you coming from?'

They check their computer. 'Ah, yes, your bag's been left behind. But it will arrive on the next flight.'

Seventy-two hours later, I'm *still* wearing the clothes I wore when boarding in Cape Town. And these people want to host the next World Cup!

My baggage and I are reconciled, about 10 hours before I'm due to fly back!

My return flight via Heathrow is cancelled. Something about a pilot overshooting the runway. Must be a former South African taxi driver . . .

BA tells me that KLM will fly me to Frankfurt and then get SAA to take me to Cape Town. I check in at their super-efficient self-service check-in counters, but then I have to stand in a queue to drop off my luggage. Thirty minutes later, the queue has moved 1.5 metres. Backwards. I go to a stewardess who advises me to go to the Business Class counter. I get there, but of course, they've *just* closed the flight!

So they send me to Lufthansa. They have a flight to Frankfurt that will make my connecting flight in time. Or that's what they told me before bad weather played its part. A German butch bitch serves us. She started just German and butch, and then turns bitch. She announces the gates for all the connecting flights for passengers on board. Except the one to Cape Town. As she passes, I say, 'Excuse me.' She just continues walking, shaking her head. What was she thinking? That I wanted her phone number? Bitch!

We're on a bus heading to the terminal to catch my connecting flight. I see it, but I don't want to believe it. The rainbow flag on the tail of a plane taxiing, about to take off. It's my connecting flight. And it's . . . gone.

[*Beat*.] The British Airways plane is cancelled. The Dutch can't get it together to let us board our planes on time. The German airline is delayed by weather. But the SAA plane, the third world, African plane, takes off on time. Go figure!

Lufthansa can get me onto a flight via Windhoek . . . Just one problem: the original ticket is British Airways, and Lufthansa can't open it. So I have to go to the BA counter, in Terminal One. I have to go through Passport Control to get to the BA counter. 'Sir, we have a problem,' says Passport Control. 'Your Schengen visa is a single-entry. You can go to the BA counter over there, but you can't come back.' I beg. I plead. And as I'm wondering whether he's holding out for a bribe, he lets me through.

I hasten to Air Namibia. I have not encountered more helpful staff. The plane is Noah's-ark vintage. The food is yesterday's boarding-house fare. The stewards are former OK Bazaars cashiers. But they're friendly. Efficient. We land at Windhoek

airport, the size of a spaza shop. But we board the plane for Cape Town and land
. . . on time.

Cape Town! Home! Yeehah! We're at Passport Control, and as sure as Mugabe
will steal an election, there's a Whinge family with their new Australian passports. [*Mimics.*] 'Look at this queue! And they want to host the World Cup!' I
breeze through Passport Control for South African passports.

I smile all the way back home. I open my luggage. [*Pause.*] Someone's been there
before me. I burst out laughing! And suddenly I get that warm feeling of famil-
iarity . . . it's a mess, but it's *our* mess. And, somehow, we always pull through!
And then I just knew . . . we're going to host the best World Cup! Ever held . . .
[*Aside.*] In Africa!

Music. End with stunning football and goals by African teams.

PLAY 3
BAFANA REPUBLIC: PENALTY SHOOTOUT (2009)

Sketch 1

TOILET CLEANER

The character is a TOILET CLEANER, *a 30-something black man, with a matric certificate. The style of the piece is, on the one hand, to talk to his 'clients' and to alternate this with speaking to the audience. He has the tools of his trade: a cloth and water bottle with a spray top. He is light, charming and funny, with everything told with a broad smile.*

CLEANER [*to audience*]: My father always told me to finish my matric so I could get a good job. He only had primary school education . . . so he worked as a labourer in the building trade. Till he passed on to that big mansion in the sky. I got my matric. And a job at the OR Tambo airport departures terminal. I wonder how my father would feel about his son being an engineer? A 'sanitary engineer' . . .

[*Sniggers.*] Big name for a toilet cleaner.

[*To a 'client'.*] Hello, sir, welcome to my boardroom. You can use cubicle number two . . . let me just wipe your throne [*as if wiping the toilet seat*] before you sit down. Enjoy it, sir. [*To another.*] Hello, boss. Allow me to turn on the tap. You can dry your hands here, chief. [*Putting out his hand to a third to accept a tip.*] Oh, thank you, sir. God bless.

[*To audience.*] You probably think this is going to be full of toilet humour. [*Reassuringly.*] Relax. It's not a Leon Schuster movie. But there are some funny things that happen here. [*Acting out some of the scenes.*] Like the guys who come in, bursting to use the loo, but it's a full house! Then you see them doing these strange things [*imitating people trying to keep in their poo*] to make sure they don't mess in their pants. I call it 'the number two shuffle'! [*Does it again, exaggeratedly.*]

But there was this one guy who actually did wet his pants. Too much coffee, he explained later. His breath did smell like coffee, with a lot of Irish! I helped him by washing his pants in the basin and then drying it under the hand-dryer while he waited in a cubicle in his yellow underpants. That used to be white. I got a big tip for that one. The notes were also full of pee, so I had to launder the money too . . .

Sometimes all five cubicles are full. *And* there's a queue. All those Wimpy breakfasts with beans now exploding . . . like an orchestra of volcanic eruptions. Those in the queue look away, embarrassed, or make like they can't hear anything, or smile nervously, knowing that they're up next. Like they're taking part in *Idols* or something. Except, the really big farts are on the outside . . . the judges.

You get all types though. There are the ones who sit on the loo and read their newspapers. My worst are those who read the *Mail & Guardian.* They sit there for hours! Fortunately, there's no wi-fi in the cubicles. Some people would set up office. And the people who talk on their cell phones. They think because *they* can't see anyone, no one can hear them. The things I've heard! The financial deals that were made. 'I'm just finishing off the paperwork now.' The breaking up. [*Mockingly.*] 'It's not you, it's me . . .'

There was this guy who was literally finishing off the paperwork [*makes as if wiping his bum*] but talking on his mobile at the same time. Resting between his shoulder and his ear. But somehow, it fell into the toilet. And it wasn't a floater. He asked me to help get the phone out. I said . . . [*puts up his hands as if he is going to say 'absolutely not'*] 'How much?'

Then there were these two George Michaels who obviously had the hots for each other. They tried to slip into one cubicle together, but I saw them through the mirror. I knocked on the door and told them that this was a family facility. And that the Mile High Club was still parked on the runway outside! They said, 'It's our constitutional right . . .' I said, 'Maybe in South Africa, but here, it's Zimbabwe!'

You can see the differences in nationalities from their toilet habits. The French never lift the seat before they pee. The British don't put down the seat afterwards. And the Germans don't wash their hands. But they tip really well. Especially when you look after their giraffes while they're doing their business. Every time a tourist does a number two, I see it as foreign direct investment. They do their job so I have mine!

This toilet is a public-private partnership. I'm an entrepreneur. It's like a tourist destination. Not exactly the Big Five. But maybe for a big number two.

It's about the experience. That's where I come in. Those three to five minutes they spend in the loo must be the best time they've ever had in a toilet. Then they'll not only tip me, but they'll come back again. And maybe send other people too.

My dream is to be the first sanitary engineer millionaire! The World Cup is going to make that happen! I'll be able to say that I've worked myself up from the *bottom*. I'll be a BEE millionaire – Bum Economic Empowerment. Maybe they'll make a movie about me . . . Bum Bog Millionaire . . .

Bollywood music. Character dances to music. Lights fade. Cartoon.

Sketch 2

ESTATE AGENT 1

The character is an ESTATE AGENT *becoming increasingly desperate to sell the Green Point stadium. She is a Sea Point kugel.*

ESTATE AGENT: Location! Location! Location! That's the bottom line, isn't it? And what better location for a football stadium than one kilometre from the sea, 50 kilometres from the townships and right next to a McDonalds? Hey?

Check out the stunning views, doll! [*Conspiratorially.*] We've managed to block everyone else's view, but this stadium has 360-degree views. Table Mountain. The Waterfront. Robben Island . . . although you can't see the actual island because of all the rabbits.

And the stadium has wonderful finishings . . . unlike Bafana's finishing at the World Cup, hey? The only time they scored, it was an own goal! But check out these finishings. The roof's from Germany. The tiles from Morocco. The showers are pure Italy. [*Aside.*] Even the grass is from . . . Swaziland!

And I don't need to point out its spaciousness. It can take 80 000 comfortably, but if you get a taxi driver to manage it, you can almost double the capacity. We haven't had much use of the stadium since the World Cup. The largest crowd since then was President Zuma's family reunion. They had it here because of the off-street parking. Ja, the 5 000 parking bays were just enough for the bodyguards.

Just think what you could do with this space . . . You could . . . you could . . . well, I don't know. You could open a zoo. [*Snorts.*] [*Aside, under her breath.*] At least you'll start with a white elephant.

With the current credit crunch, the stadium is a superb investment. [*Beat.*]

No, I mean it! All around the world they'll still be having Olympic Games, football World Cups and rock concerts, right? But no one's going to be able to afford new stadiums anymore, so you could rent out this one. Lease it to London for the 2012 Olympics! Earn some pounds, doll!

And yes, it's very secure. Okay, so the Italians were robbed in the semi-finals, but since then we haven't had a problem with crime. And it's got its own generators . . . so it's an Eskom-free facility.

The price? Well, it's as good as new! It's only been used for five football games! It cost us 4 billion, but we're selling it – not for 5 billion, not for 4.5 billion. Not even for 4 billion. We're practically giving it away for 3 billion. In fact, we're paying you to buy it from us.

2.5 billion? 2? 1.5? Okay, okay, I see. So can I interest you in something else maybe? There's a lovely little semi, also in Green Point. It has great views of the stadium . . . great views.

Lights fade. Screen comes to life with some of the best goals from the recent Africa Cup.

Sketch 3

FALSE PROPHET

The character is a 50-plus PREACHER *who talks to the audience – his congregation – in the style of a southern American preacher or in Martin Luther King style. He wipes the sweat off his forehead as he preaches.*

PREACHER: Brothers and sisters-a, some call me a false prophet-a, but they are the ones who say that you, the poor-a, shall always be with us-a! But today, I bring you tidings of great joy-a! For the good news-a is that the FIFA World Cup, brothers and sisters-a, shall deliver you from your poverty-a!

I know that I once told you to believe in the arms deal-a! That submarines and jets and corvettes will deliver houses, and jobs, and security, and comfort-a! And for some, it did-a! Look at Brother Schabir Shaik, brothers and sisters-a. He was *secure* in Westville Prison-a! He was *comfortable* in Durban hospitals-a!

But, my dear brothers and sisters-a, if the arms deal brought benefits for some-a, it is the FIFA World Cup-a that will save you all from the damnation of poverty-a! That will deliver you from the hell of your townships and squatter camps-a, and take you to heaven, to a land flowing with milk and honey . . . to . . . Khayelitsh-a!

Yes, brothers and sisters-a! I have been to the mountain-a! [*hinting at initiation*] and I have become a man-a! And then I went to the top of the mountain-a! And from there, I saw the Promised Land-a! And in it was Green Point stadium-a! Brothers and sisters-a . . . we promised you jobs-a, health-a, education-a, houses-a, and we gave you . . . the FIFA World Cup-a!

In the past-a, it was said that religion was the opiate of the masses-a. But today, brothers and sisters-a, it is not religion-a! It is not television-a! Certainly not SATV, where there is more drama in the boardroom than on our screens-a! I don't mind telling you this-a, but today's opiate of the masses-a is . . . sport-a! Rugby-a! Cricket-a! Football-a!

Which is why we are giving you the FIFA World Cup-a!

When you wait in that queue to have your sick child seen to at the clinic-a, just believe in the World Cup-a! When you stand by the side of the road waiting for someone to give you a job-a, just believe in the World Cup-a! When you don't have food to feed your family-a, when it rains and your shack is under water-a! When you have no money to send your children to school-a, just watch football-a!

There's a good thing coming, brothers and sisters-a! And it will save you from all your misery. The world is not going to end-a! No, brothers and sisters-a, your new world-a, our new world-a, will start on the 11th of June 2010-a! It will be the dawn of houses for all! Jobs for everyone! No more crime-a! And no more taxi drivers-a!

So, in closing, brothers and sisters-a, we are taking up a collection for the FIFA World Cup today-a. [*Aside.*] And for the next 20 years! [*To audience.*] Dig deep into your pockets, brothers and sisters-a. Give generously. For it is in your giving that a few of us shall receive! Amen!

Sketch 4

MADONNA OF AFRICA

The character is a MADONNA-*like singer. She is hosting a press conference to launch an international adoption agency. She sings in between talking to the audience.*

MADONNA [*enters, hands in the air, singing to the tune of Michael Jackson's 'We Are the World'*]:

We are the world, we are the children . . .
We are the ones to make a better day
So let's start giving . . .
We are the world . . .

MADONNA [*acknowledging the applause*]: Thank you, thank you. I want to thank the media, my fans and all my fellow celebrities – Oprah, Bono [*gritting her teeth*], Angelina [*under her breath*] . . . bitch! [*back to a big smile*] for coming to the launch of Celebrity Adoptions of Children for Africa . . . [*Beat.*]

CACA.

We're here today because Mother Africa has so many children. And Father Africa has deserted her.

When I first visited Africa . . . through Google Earth . . . I was surprised to see how big it was. Then, when I actually visited the place to get the one thing I didn't have – a photo with Nelson Mandela – the flight was taking so long, I said to the pilot, just stop at the next airport. That's how I landed up in Malawi. And I'm glad I did. Better Mal-awi than Mal-ema . . .

Anyway, it was there that I heard about all these orphans . . . genocide orphans, AIDS orphans, liberation struggle orphans, taxi orphans. Aw-ful! And I knew I just had to do something. [*False smile.*] That, and because I saw how much publicity Angelina was getting from all her adoptions! [*Aside again.*] Bitch!

So I took some money out of my marketing and publicity budget and bought . . . sorry, adopted . . . a child. Right there and then. David. Beautiful African name.

[*She then speaks the words of the first two verses of her song 'Like a Virgin'.*]

I was a bit
Incomplete
Though I'd been had so many times
I was sad and blue
But David made me feel
Yeah, David made me feel
Shiny and new

[*She sings the chorus, her tone and almost nun-like movements in contrast to the racy words.*]

Like a virgin
Touched for the very first time
Like a virgin
When your heart beats
Next to mine

There are so many children in Africa looking for a home! So I would like to challenge all my fellow artists to adopt African children . . . Bob Dylan, Lionel Ritchie, Michael Jackson . . . okay, maybe not Michael Jackson.

Mother Africa has given us Obama. It is only right that we give something back. These countries are in such debt, we can each adopt a country! Bono can have Botswana. Geldof can adopt Ghana . . . And because his music is among the most pirated, Michael Jackson can have Somalia.

[*She sings, swaying from side to side with her hands in the air, with the lights fading slowly and with a lighter in hand.*]

Feed the world
Let them know it's Christmastime
Even though most Africans are Muslim . . .

Lights fade. Appropriate cartoon/s up on screen.

Sketch 5

DISABLED

Character is a 30-something ATHLETE – *he has a leg crippled by polio. He walks with difficulty and uses a crutch, which he also uses in the sketch as sporting equipment.*

Lights come up as the actor walks on stage so everyone can see him.

ATHLETE *goes through his weightlifting routine. First he uses the crutch as a dumb-bell in one hand, counting to 10, and then in the other hand. Then he uses it as if it is a heavy weight, lifting it up above his head with both hands. Throughout, he engages with the audience, smiling and making them laugh with his physical antics.*

The South African national anthem begins to play.

ATHLETE *holds the crutch in front of him, carrying it as if it is a flagpole.*

The anthem fades.

ATHLETE [*facing audience*]: I'm practising for the Paralympics. [*Does dumb-bell lift again.*] Swimming. I'm going to be the first black swimming champion. At the Paralympics. That's why I like the new South Africa. Anything's possible. Even for the challenged. The intellectually challenged can become MPs. The morally challenged can be priests. And those who can't play . . . can become sports administrators.

I'm thinking of becoming an activist for disability. I want to be the Zackie Achmat of disability. And let down the tyres of all those Mercedes and BMWs that park in disabled bays. Pricks!

Did you know that 5 per cent of our population is disabled? And the most affected province is the Free State. Don't ask me why. But the Free State Cheetahs are at the bottom of the Super 14 log, so it must be true.

You're probably wondering how I got like this. Maybe you're thinking taxi accident? Or gang shooting? Or rugby tackle? Actually, I was chasing after a BEE deal, and I tripped over Cyril.

I'm not too worried. Best thing that ever happened to me. Now I qualify for affirmative action on two counts. And for a disability grant. My neighbour wants to take me to Rhema. He assured me they don't let Carl Niehaus take the collection anymore. And he said they pray for the sick . . . they could cure my disability. [*Snorts.*] If you're on disability, why would you want to get healed? Especially in a recession?

But I'm not a hand-out kind of guy. I want to do something really useful. Like the Paralympics. Our disabled athletes do so much better than our able-bodied.

That's why I think they should let disabled people run the country. I mean, everyone's going on about Zuma. They tell us he's only got a Standard 6 education. He's morally challenged, they say. He's not presidential, they moan. They make out like he's completely disabled!

But look at the guy before him. Intellectual. But he didn't know that HIV causes AIDS. And now thousands of people are dead. He's such a bright spark, but he didn't know they needed more electricity plants to drive the economy. He was so clever that we had the biggest rate of unemployment, and the widest gap between rich and poor, when he was president. Under him we had the worst crime, and the Zimbabwe Ruins went national.

And no, I'm not looking for a job. I don't want to be in Zuma's cabinet. I mean, imagine having to go to fortnightly meetings with Nkosazana Zuma?

All I'm saying is that maybe someone who's not perfect, who's flawed – like the rest of us – will be humbler. A bit more caring. And listen more.

Our trophy cupboard can be so much fuller! I say, bring on the disabled.

Music, appropriate cartoons.

Sketch 6

JIMMY BLOND

The character, JIMMY BLOND, *is a 40-something, been-through-the-mill, street-wise, Afrikaans-speaking guy who thinks he's cool. He uses many of the names of Bond movies as part of the sketch. The sentences are short and punchy, indicating the manic style that the sketch should be played in.*

James Bond movie theme music.

Enter actor wearing a blond wig and suit.

BLOND: The name's Blond. Jimmy Blond. Code 00-2-7-21-531-6749. [*Takes traditional phone receiver out of his pocket.*] Hello there, Jimmy here . . . how may I direct your call? Joost? [*Snorts.*] [*To audience, referencing Joost saying that it wasn't him in the video as 'that man was better hung'.*] *The Man with the* – short – *Golden Gun*! [*Into the phone.*] What can I do you for? You want me to find who leaked that video? I'm sorry . . . I'm a private detective, not a private *parts* investigator! That video should have been *for your eyes only*, scrumbag! [*Puts the phone down.*] Besides, I'm busy. [*Conspiratorially, to audience.*] I'm on contract to Helen Zille. That's right! I'm *on Her Majesty's Secret Service*. My assignment? No, not to find a woman for her cabinet, or a concubine for her bed, but to find out who leaked the botox story.

James Bond movie theme music.

First stop. The plastic surgeon. A black cat runs across my path. I swerve. And almost make peanut butter. It loses one life. But *Octopussy* lives to *die another day*. The surgeon's [*cups his two hands under his breasts*] loaded. *A view to kill* for . . . ! Her melons may be temporary, but her bling-bling *diamonds are forever*. [*With a suggestive pelvic movement.*] I can't say I'm not stirred! This could get interesting. I check the bathroom for protection. Yes! It has a shower! But, business first. [*Interrogatively.*] Did she leak the story? No. Does she know who did? No. Does she think I'm sexy? No. *Dr No* sends me on my way, this time with her bling *gold finger*. [*Shows his right middle finger.*]

James Bond movie theme music.

I drive away. Deep in thought. Then it strikes me. This could be an inside job. Tony Leon! He's travelling the globe since he resigned. But maybe . . . *the world is not enough.* Maybe he doesn't like Helen getting so much press. *Live and let die* . . . like his hair. No, that would be too easy. And the sketch would end now. And I've only worked through half the Bond movie titles!

James Bond movie theme music.

I hear a whistle. I turn around. I find myself staring into the eyes of Arletta Louisa Terreblanche, *the spy who loved me* when she and I worked for the Bureau of State Security. For her, *tomorrow never dies.* She dreams that one day we'll ride off into the sunset together. The very thought makes me fart. Like a *thunderball.* She smiles adoringly through her crooked teeth and scares *the living daylights* out of me! I run like hell.

James Bond movie theme music.

Everywhere's a dead end. I need to find a politician. Who'll talk. For a few quick bucks! I make my way to a strip joint, the *Casino Royale.* The girls are *from Russia . . . with love.* Just as I thought. The Home Affairs portfolio committee is here . . . to study the patterns [*makes hourglass shape with his hands*] of immigration. I lay my cards on the table. They give me the *golden eye.* 'Cash only. No credit cards. And no more travel vouchers.' [*Shrugs his shoulders, wryly.*] That was useful . . . !

James Bond movie theme music.

Next, I *steak out* the journalist who broke the news. She's hot. '*Well done,*' I tune her. I get to the point. 'Who's your *sauce?*' She *peppers* me with foul language. I'm not shaken. Before you can say '*quantum of solace*', she's off to expose Niehaus . . . leaving him . . . kaal. In politics, *you only live twice.* Once as a liar. Twice as a fraudster. That hack's on a mission. She's a *moon* . . . no, a mud*raker* . . . with a *licence to kill* . . . political careers!

I'm in the wrong business! I should be . . . in the media!

Bond music. Lights fade. Music. Cartoon.

Sketch 7

SCHOOL FOR AFRICAN DICTATORS

The character is a LECTURER *in his 50s, suave, charming on the outside, but just below the surface is a ruthless streak. He smiles a lot, only to stop smiling abruptly. He lectures with a cane in hand. Use can be made of the screen to project images that reinforce, contradict or just add humour to the lecture.*

LECTURER: Good morning, gentlemen, and welcome to the African Union's exclusive course: Dictators 101. You are here because you have won wars of liberation against the colonialists, the imperialists, the McDonald's globalists. In doing so, you have *earned* the right to oppress and abuse your own people.

Gentlemen – [*with a wry smile*] and the not-so-*gentle*-men among you – in accordance with our African Renaissance Public Relations project, the African Union would like to project an image of peace and stability, democracy and rationality to the outside world. For this reason, we have chosen as our leader for the next period the Honourable, the One and Only, the *Other* Special One, Colonel Gaddafi.

This is the African century! We will be hosting the football World Cup for the first time. And just because football has its roots in a colonial power doesn't mean we reject football. In the same way that we don't reject champagne simply because it is French, right?

We are convinced that an African team will win the World Cup for the first time . . . For we are saying to FIFA that because of what the West did to Africa – slavery, apartheid, introducing hip hop – we demand compensation. All African teams will start every game with a two-goal advantage. Except Bafana. They will start with four goals. Shame.

For the first time ever, there is an African in the White House. There are the Afro-pessimists who say you can take the African out of Africa, but you can't take Africa out of the African. So they're all expecting Obama to mess up America – and the world. As if anyone can do worse than George Bush.

Which is why, gentlemen, we are running this course. To help Obama. We can no longer be a factory for trials at the International Court of Justice! Which is not to say you can no longer loot state coffers. It is rather a question of 'how'. That is why we will teach you how to be a modern, African Renaissance dictator. How to have your cake . . . and the whole damn bakery!

Now is the time to project the African way into the global order. In the West, the one with the most votes becomes president. We must teach them the humbler African way . . . the loser becomes president, the winner, prime minister.

Gentlemen, let us learn from the West. They do far worse things than us, but they don't land up on trial in The Hague. George Bush almost starts World War III and all he gets is a shoe thrown at him. Tony Blair supports the murder of thousands of Iraqis. And now he's the special envoy to solve the problems of the Middle East!

We're doing something wrong! I ask you to look, not to the West, but to the South. Our esteemed Comrade Mbeki has killed off hundreds of thousands of South Africans. Is he on trial in The Hague? No! Why? Because, gentlemen, he may be African and black, but he looks and talks like the West.

So, in this course, you will no longer learn to kill and loot and rule with an AK-47. But to do so with poetry.

Sketch 8

DOG SHRINK

The character is not a kugel. She is a 35-year-old white LIBERAL MUM *with two children, the eldest of whom is a son,* DANIEL, *in Grade 10. He attends an upmarket single-sex school. She genuinely thinks that she is quite progressive and 'new South African'. Here she is speaking to an animal behaviourist.*

LIBERAL MUM: It was my friend Melissa who told me about you . . . you can always rely on Melissa Giles-Thompson. Everyone in our book club has a personal trainer, a plastic surgeon and a marriage counsellor, but trust Melissa to have a dog psychologist as well! She says you did wonders for her poodle. He doesn't hump the imported cushions anymore. Just her husband's leg. [*Laughs.*]

I really hope you can help me. It's quite embarrassing, actually. I mean, it's 2009 [*half-embarrassed*] and our dog still only barks at black people. [*Beat.*]

She's only two years old, so it's not like she knows anything about apartheid.

And the thing is, *she's* black! At least on the outside! My husband teases her and calls her Coconut. But her name's actually Coco. Do you think . . . *she* thinks she's white? I mean, during the elections, she barked at people who put ANC pamphlets in our letter-box, but wagged her tail when they were DA pamphlets.

And she hates Zimbabweans. She just barks normally for other blacks, but for Zimbabweans, I swear she barks [*imitating a bark*] 'Amakwerekwere, amakwerekwere'. We used to have a Zimbabwean gardener. He was such a good worker. Much better than *our* blacks, who are a little lazy, full of HIV and prone to violence. Anyway, Coco hated him so much we had to change him for a retrenched white banker who started this landscaping business . . . Ag shame, we felt so sorry for him! [*Pause.*] No . . . for the banker.

Whenever my son Daniel plays his black music, Coco whines so loud and so long you'd think it was Terror Lekota. But when we put on Lloyd Webber, she just lies there . . . with a big smile on her face.

It's not that we mind her barking at blacks . . . It's good if they're scared of her. But it makes Daniel really cross. He doesn't want to bring his black school friends home anymore. When they did come here, I was amazed . . . they could all swim! So now he's always sleeping out at *their* homes over weekends. And we don't know what he gets up to with them. It's bad enough that when he dances [*gets up to illustrate*] he holds his crotch. And everything is like 'eish' and 'aweh'. And now he wants to give up French for Xhosa. It's like he's changing from a thoroughbred to a mongrel!

Look, I have no problem with the school being open to everyone. [*Changes tone.*] The only thing is . . . some of these new parents want to introduce soccer at the school. It's crazy. My son's school has always been a *rugby* school! My husband went there. His father went there. And *his* father. And you know what? They all played in the C team! You don't just mess with tradition! I mean, if you want to play soccer, why come to *our* school when you know it's a rugby school?

I got *so* angry at a parents' meeting the other day . . . there was this parent going on and on about football. I nearly threw my shoe at him. I'm glad I didn't. I found out afterwards he's a BEE billionaire who owns a football team.

The thing is, why would any boy *want* to play football? I mean, look at Bafana Bafana! There's no incentive to play for them.

And if the school offered soccer, we would attract a lower-class boy. I'm sorry, but just because we're open to everyone doesn't mean we have to lower our standards or our values. Because it's not just soccer. It's the whole culture around it! The drugs. The pregnant teenagers. The losing! And the fighting on and off the field. When they come to our schools, they must understand that it's on our terms. And it's our responsibility to bring them up to our standards.

Okay, look, I know some people will point to Bishops, where the matrics trashed the school at the end of last year . . . and they play rugby. But just *think* what they would have done if they played football!

And can you imagine having to deal with the opposition's parents . . . especially from the lower classes. I mean, it's bad enough when our rugby teams have to play against some Dutchman school and get absolutely thrashed while their parents braai on the side . . . like it's Vlakplaas or something. Imagine having to go into the townships to watch your child play football . . . and everyone is on tik!

Sorry, I know I'm going on . . . but here's the thing. My husband wants to bring his new boss home for dinner. He's black. *And* he's Zimbabwean! So you understand my problem. I've tried everything. I've taken Coco to what I thought was a Model C dog school . . . where she can socialise properly. I've even tried to make her feel more black by feeding her Kentucky bones. But she nearly choked . . .

My husband thinks it will impress his boss if Daniel is at the dinner with some of his black friends . . . since we don't have any. Yet. But now you can see why Coco's the problem. Can you help?

Lights fade. Music and appropriate cartoons.

PLAY 4
PAY BACK THE CURRY (2016)

Sketch 1

TIME TRAVEL

Essentially, in this sketch the character is a TOUR GUIDE, *with the audience as passengers on his time-travel machine. He moves (slowly but constantly) like an astronaut floating in a capsule. When he speaks, he does so dreamily.*

The actor is on stage as audience arrives.

The lights come up.

TOUR GUIDE: Welcome aboard our time-travel machine.

First, we travel to a land of the future
Where scrums are reserved for the rugby field, not Parliament
Where jobs are desperate for matriculants
And dogs also bark at white people

Let me take you to a museum
It is only there that you will see
Black pain and
White privilege
For ubuntu and equity are now easy bedfellows
And black people are genuinely happy
Even in Cape Town

Let us walk along un-littered streets
Named after flora and fauna
Rather than fawning some flawed victor
And living monuments are the people whose dignity
Has been affirmed with
Spacious houses
A plot of land
Safe neighbourhoods

And taxis have been smelted
Into public art

Come with me to the world-class stadium
To watch the national rugby team
With its six black forwards and its one white wing
The three-quarters Blacks beating the All Blacks . . . again

Stay on to watch the fully transformed
National soccer team
Now replete with Somalians, Zimbabweans, Congolese
The much-loved
Bafana Kwere Kwere
Ranked number one in Africa

It is a land in which electric fences
Have been exiled by welcoming lawns
Where women walk freely
And return home without fear
Where corruption is manifest only
In computer software

In this future land
The president is a woman
Who speaks Afrikaans . . .
And Pedi, Sotho and Zulu
She serves not a family
Not a party
But the people

[*Change in tone/mood.*]

Now travel back in time with me
To another country
When black people had more passes between them
Than today's matriculants

Forced from the land
By law
By gun

To offer
Their bodies to the violence of
Cheap labour
On farms
Down mines
In kitchens
Sacrificed on the altar of white privilege
The collateral damage of white affirmative action

For you reluctant history tourists
Close your eyes
Shut your ears
Harden your heart
And deny the logic of institutional theft
Comfort yourself that all that you have
Is because of hard work
Superior intelligence
God's rich blessings

[*Change in tone, more upbeat, but between the future and the past.*]

Now let's travel to the in-between land
Where the past is with us
As we seek to sow
The future before us

The war has stopped
But the battles have begun
It is a land of paradox
Of more schools and less education
More millionaires but not less poverty
More crime, less punishment
More growth, fewer jobs
More hospitals, poorer health
Fewer race laws
More race incidents

A time of tension
Better than the past

But not yet the future
Had enough?
Good! Let's go
Back to the future!

[*Actor struggles to move forward to where the future was earlier; it is as if he's stuck.*]

Oh no!

[*Speaks into a radio.*] Houston, we have a problem . . .

[*To audience, as if they are the passengers.*]

Please bear with us.
We have a technical problem.
It seems that we'll be stuck in the present for a bit.
We will have to use local transport.

Sketch 2

FLY SAA

The character is an AIRLINE STEWARD, *making on-board announcements. The director and actor can determine the best form to use, but the text should be played as straight as possible. S/he is polite, enthusiastic and yet, with a sense of irony, aware that s/he has to do her/his job, while also being aware of the ambivalence of some of what s/he is saying.*

AIRLINE STEWARD: Good evening and welcome aboard South African Airways, Boeing, Boeing, Boing!!! Our pilot today is Captain Jacob Zuma, who graduated from Robben Island University with *flying* colours. His co-pilot in the sucking cock pit is Dudu Myeni. Navigation is provided by the Gupta brothers and the flight plan has been devised at the Saxonwold shebeen. Our flight engineer is seconded by Eskom. This is your one-way flight to Planet Zupta, your junket to status . . . junk. Planet Zupta is the world's very first curried banana republic. And, if you think that's racist, we have yet to receive complaints from . . . bananas.

For your own safety, we advise you to leave this aircraft now.

[*Pumps up his body as if a bouncer, looks around intimidatingly, and before anyone can move, he proceeds, relaxing his body.*]

My name is Give-or-Take Myeni-Zuma; I am the purser on this flight, which means that I help myself to your wallets while you sleep. The crew on this flight has been redeployed from Correctional Services for allegedly accepting bribes, but that was really just a simple misunderstanding between Western law and African culture.

In the interests of national security, please switch off all your electronic equipment, or we will be obliged to switch on our signal jammer.

Business Class is, of course, reserved for the ANC, as they come first. If you're in Economy Class, please use the toilets in Economy Class, unless you are a pantytrepeneur, in which case you are welcome to use the ANC . . . sorry, Business Class toilets. Please indicate with which minister you would like to be tender.

On our Business Class menu, we will be serving roasted Thuli Madonsela, prepared by chef Busisiwe Mkhwebane, the new Presidential Protector. Passengers will be provided with real knives and forks because Thuli Madonsela is very tough. For starters, Business Class will have the DA with white whine, and dessert will be red EFF cherry-picked Constitutional Court judgments.

In Economy Class, we will be serving the usual three courses: promises, spin and denial. There is no T-bone steak, no rump steak, just mis-takes. All served on a bed of white monopoly capital.

On today's flight, we do have the chicken or beef option, now known as the Nene or Van Rooyen. [*Walks straight as if down a plane aisle, offering options.*] Nene or Van Rooyen? Nene or Van Rooyen? What's the difference? This one . . . the Van Rooyen . . . is more qualified than this one . . . to send you straight down the toilet!

So fasten your seat belt by inserting the clip into the buckle. When you hear the click, don't worry, it's just Mmusi Maimane practising his Xhosa.

Captain Zuma has informed us that we'll be cruising at an altitude of 13 thousand, 40 million and 20 hundred feet. [*Beat.*]

[*As if listening again.*] Make that 20 thousand, 13 million and 40 hundred feet. Whatever.

Our in-flight newspapers, the *Independent* and *New Age*, are made available to you freely thanks to public sector advertising; in other words, your captured taxes. In-flight entertainment is provided by the Parliamentary Channel, which also doubles as the Crime Channel and the Cartoon Network.

In the likely event of the flight losing altitude as fast as the rand, oxygen masks will automatically be lowered in Business Class. For the rest of you, don't overreact, there's Sudoku in the *New Age* to take your mind off things.

Flight control has informed us of a few thunderstorms ahead, at least until 2019, or until the captain is recalled. They also say that due to social media turbulence, it is necessary to keep your seat belts fastened.

In the event of an emergency, Business Class passengers and the crew have been equipped with parachutes.

If you are seated next to an emergency exit, please get out of the way so that Business Class passengers can get out first. In such instances, blue lights will light up towards the exits.

Please note that this is a non-smoking flight; that's because it is now powered by nuclear energy, so called because it will help to support the captain's nuclear family.

Speaking of which, in the seat pocket in front of you, you will find an envelope to make a contribution to the charity supported by our airline. We all know that charity begins at home, so your contributions will go straight towards the Nkaaandla Family Foundation.

Sit back, relax and enjoy being taken for a ride.

Sketch 3

FALLISM

The character is the HOST *of a discussion-type TV programme interviewing university students* BANTU, ZUBEIDA, SIMON, KOLEKA *and* RIAAN.

Typical television news-type musical introduction plays.

HOST: In this week's edition of *News Night,* we discuss the topic of 'fallism'! We are delighted to have in studio five young leaders to speak about the 'Must Fall' student movement that has swept the country in recent times.

From the University of KwaZulu-Natal, we have Koleka Ngubane, who's doing her third-year BA, the acronym for Blame Apartheid studies. Next to her is University of Cape Town's Simon Osmond, a PhD – or Privileged Homosexual Discourse – student. Riaan van Schalkwyk is from the University of the Free State, where he is doing his MA – [*in Afrikaans*] My Afrikaans or [*in English*] My Afrikaans . . . that's right, he's doing it bilingually. Bantu Mphahlele is a student leader who's also doing his BA – Burn Art – in Cape Town. Zubeida Aslam is a second-year Bachelor of State Capture – or BSC – student at UWC.

So, let's get straight into it. While the student movement has been talking the language of decolonisation on their campuses, some would say that the country has actually been recolonised by a family from India. They've come in, captured our president and a few strategic ministers, and are extracting our wealth and repatriating it abroad.

BANTU: That is such a white perspective.

HOST: But I'm black.

BANTU: Only on the outside. Fanon warned us about people like you. Black skin, white masks, grey suit.

HOST: Why is that a 'white' perspective, Bantu? After all, this was the gist of the Public Protector's report on state capture.

BANTU: Blacks cannot be colonisers. Only whites can colonise.

ZUBEIDA: I agree with my brother Bantu. Black people don't colonise. They can only decolonise.

BANTU: Like blacks cannot be racist.

SIMON [*ironically*]: When they are, it's called 'xenophobia'.

HOST: So, is this all a matter of terminology? The effect is the same, but depending on the colour of those doing it, we call it different things?

KOLEKA: Ja, blacks 'murder', white people 'commit culpable homicide'.

RIAAN: Ek wil net sê ... I just want to say ... Engels must fall. English moet val. Engels is colonial. Afrikaans is indigenous.

BANTU: Afrikaans is the language of exclusion ...

RIAAN: It's not true ... dis nie waar nie. We're just claiming our constitutional right to learn in our language. Ons ...

HOST: Okay, Riaan, we get it.

ZUBEIDA: Afrikaans was actually the language of slaves ...

RIAAN: Ja, but the slaves belonged to us, so it was okay for us to take their language.

KOLEKA: I also have the constitutional right to learn in my mother tongue, but thanks to apartheid, neither my mother nor my tongue has a university.

RIAAN: The British did bad things to all of us, but here we are, speaking Engels ...

HOST: I want us to come back to the topic. Some people say that the Must Fall movement is the work of a Third Force.

SIMON: It started with shit being thrown at a statue. So it was certainly started by a turd force.

HOST: There was a lot of criticism of the Must Fall movement when students burned art, saying that this was a sign of barbarism!

BANTU: And what do they call the people who burn sculptures at AfrikaBurn?

SIMON: Er, white?

KOLEKA: Art is not neutral. Art can take sides.

HOST: And if it takes the wrong side, it must be destroyed?

KOLEKA: Even UCT agreed to remove Rhodes's statue because of what it represented.

RIAAN: Burning art ... removing statues ... we're heading towards un-civilisation.

ZUBEIDA: Like when the apartheid government banned music, plays and festivals?

RIAAN: Ons moet die verlede vergeet. We must forget the past. And move on.

HOST: How do you respond to those who say that 'fallism' is inherently destructive and that it doesn't build anything?

SIMON: To build a better society, some things must first fall. Racism must fall. Patriarchy must fall. Homophobia must fall. Fallism resists all oppressions.

BANTU: But first and foremost, racism must fall. We mustn't complicate the struggle of the black man with issues like homophobia. That's the issue of a privileged white minority . . . it's part of our colonisation.

SIMON: That is SO Zuma . . . !

KOLEKA: What about the struggle of the black *woman*?

ZUBEIDA: I agree with my brother Bantu . . . given our apartheid history, our primary struggle is for the liberation of black people from white racism.

RIAAN: So they can be exploited by Indians?

HOST: Riaan, thula . . .

KOLEKA: So it's okay for black men to oppress women and the LGBTI community as long as they are struggling against racism?

BANTU: The whites must first give blacks our land.

ZUBEIDA: And then the blacks can give the land back to the Khoi and the San.

BANTU: What?

ZUBEIDA: We were here first.

BANTU: But, Zubeida, we're all black. Just like Biko says.

ZUBEIDA: We're only black enough when it suits you, Bantu.

BANTU: Zubeida, we must unite against people like Simon.

SIMON: I'm sorry, I can't work with homophobes.

BANTU: That's okay, I can't work with whites.

KOLEKA: I don't work with sexists, of any colour.

RIAAN: Fok Engels. Come work with me in Afrikaans, Zubeida.

ZUBEIDA: So now I'm white enough for you . . . voetsek!

HOST: Well, ladies and gentlemen, that's all we have time for. One thing for which we don't need the colonisers any longer is to divide and rule us. We are quite capable of doing that ourselves. Goodnight!

Sketch 4

AND THE OSCAR GOES TO . . .

Actor imitates OSCAR PISTORIUS. *He is on his knees, as if his blades are off. He has an anxious, high-pitched voice.*

OSCAR: Ladies and gentlemen, welcome to the Femicide Oscars.

In the category for Best Screenplay, the nominees are:

Barry Roux for *Yes, My Lady*
Barry Roux for *As You Please, My Lady*
Barry Roux for *My Lady, My Lady*
Barry Roux for *My Very Fair Lady*
Gerrie Nel for *See You at the Court of Appeal*

The nominees for the Best Foreign Language movie are:

Persona Non Grata
Dolus Eventualis
My Cellmate, Radovan Krejcir

In the Science Fiction category, the nominees are:

Blade Runner Goes to Jail
Blade Runner Goes to Jail 2
Blade Must Fall [*Shakes his head.*] Sorry, that was a late entry.

The Best Sound Effects category has three nominees:

Screaming like a girl
Shots like a cricket bat
Vomiting like a dog

Vying for honours in the Animated Movie category are the following nominees:

Tall Story
Beauty and the Beast
Despicable Me

The three movies nominated in the Horror category are:

The Bucket List [*Vomits into a bucket.*]
While You Were Sleeping, and . . .
We Know What You Did Last Valentine's Day!

Sounds of four gunshots. OSCAR *reacts. Lets out a little cry.*

I've been asked to read a message from our sponsors:

'The Oscars are not just white this year, or any South African year
For five times the global average . . .
Every eight hours . . .
Three times a day
A woman is killed by her intimate partner.'

Finally, while we are all equal before the law, it is those with money who often get away with murder. So, in the category for the Best Original Song, the sole nominee is an ABBA remake:

'Money, Money, Money . . . can't buy you freedom'. [*Vomits.*]

Sketch 5

BORN FREE

The character is THANDI, *a contestant in* The Voiceless *talent show.*

THANDI: Hello, my name's Thandi. For my audition for *The Voiceless* [*giggles*] I'll be singing 'Born Free'.

[*Sings to the tune of the popular song 'Born Free'.*]

Born free, but born into poverty
Planned a good story
My parents had hopes for me

UCT, where I wanted to be
But no funds for Model C
I passed matric with an E

Falling fees, great for those at varsity
But what of the rest, what of our life's quest?

Born free, but is life worth living
If poor and no prospects
Are you born free?

I thank you.

Sketch 6

WEEKEND SPECIAL

The character, DES BLESSER VAN ROOYEN, *is a contestant in the TV reality show* Idols.

DES: Hello, my name's Des Blesser van Rooyen, and for my *Idols* audition, I'll be doing a love song.

[*To the tune of Brenda Fassie's song 'Weekend Special'.*]

You say come around, to see you in Saxonwold
You're busy on the phone, laughing with Putin
The Guptas welcome me, they make me feel at home
They offer me a Coke, and a ministry

It's Friday night, yes I know, yes I know
That's when ministers are made, when ministers are made

I'm your weekend, weekend special
I'm your weak rand, weak rand special
I'm your weekend, weekend special
I'm your weak rand, weak rand special!

You say Nene is heading to Shanghai
The Guptas wink at me, we all know it's just spin
Next day I go shopping for a car and suit
With Anil telling me my job description

It's Monday night and the markets crash
Next thing I know, I'm minister of local government

I'm your weekend, weekend special
I'm your weak rand, weak rand special
I'm your weekend, weekend special
I'm your weak rand, weak rand special!

[*Repeat.*]

I'm your weekend, weekend special
I'm your weak rand, weak rand special
I'm your weekend, weekend special
I'm your weak rand, weak rand special!

Sketch 7

I AM AN AFRICAN

The character is FARAI, *a performance poet, on stage at a poetry festival.*

FARAI: Good evening. My name's Farai, and I'm from Zimbabwe. Thank you for the opportunity to perform in the Thabo Mbeki Poetry Festival.

[*Clears throat.*]

I am an African
I owe my being to the hills and valleys
The mountains and the glades
The rivers, the deserts, the trees and
The ever-changing seasons that define one face of my native continent

From which I would flee if I had the means
Am thinking of fleeing
Have now fled

For another face is of power incontinents
A president for life in Harare
Killer presidents in Khartoum, Nairobi, Bujumbura
A thief president in Pretoria
Rulers without shame
Now I am a president – without the P – abroad

Once taken to lands far away
In chains against my will
Now refused entry to selfsame lands
As someone free
Yet not free to travel freely

Still, I am a professor in New York
A musician in Paris
A footballer in Spain
A car guard in Cape Town
I am an African

I'm a pin-up girl for famine
A poster boy for AIDS
A cover girl for terror
The face of a charity concert
Though made faint by Syrian tears

I'm a runaway from hunger
An asylum seeker from war
A self-imposed exile from poverty
A refugee from false prophets of a better life
Now reserved for only a few

My body tells horror stories
Of white violence
Of black hatred
Of green envy
Of red ideology
Of rainbow-coloured exclusion
Of orange flames
Of silver bullets
And rusted brown machetes
I am an African

I'm an optimist, I'm a pessimist
A socialist, a capitalist
An idealist, a pragmatist
A revolutionary
A conformist
I love, I live, I laugh, I cry
I hurt, I weep, I get sick, I die
I'm black, I'm blacker and then some
I am an African

But see me foremost
See me first
See me as a human

I thank you.

Sketch 8

ESTATE AGENT 2

The character is PENNY, *a female estate agent, perhaps played with a bit of a kugel accent.*

PENNY: Hello, Jawitz No Fine Estate Agents, Penny-for-your-Noughts speaking, how may I help you find your exclusive suburb?

Yes, sir, we have the widest selection of properties in Cape Town, although we do concentrate on the *cleaner* suburbs. [*Beat.*]

Sir, you sound foreign, so could you please spell your name for me? R-O-B-E-R-T, yes, Robert, and then . . . M, yes, A-T-H-I-B-E. Robert Mathibe . . . [*Pronounces 'Mathibe' to rhyme with 'tribe'.*] Is that Portuguese, sir? [*Is corrected over the phone to pronounce it Ma-tee-beh.*] Oh! Mathibe . . . [*Pulls a face.*] Sotho? No, no, no, no problem, Mr Metaab, some of my best friends are Sothos. [*Laughs nervously, scratches under her arm.*] [*Aside, puts her hand over the receiver of the phone.*] I just haven't met them yet.

I'm sure we have a whole litter of Sothos here in Ape Town . . . I mean . . . a lotta Sothos here in Cape Town. We try to help them find places close to each other . . . Just like Mother Nature teaches us. Sparrows of a feather flock together . . . and all that.

Yes, no, I love Sothos. We even had one cleaning up after us when we lived in Joburg. At the end of every year, all the girl wanted to do was get away from our clean house and go to Durban to dirty the beaches there! But now we're very happy with our Malawian. She's not legal, so we don't have to pay the minimum salary.

But enough of me . . . Mr Metaabeh, tell me, do you have little monkeys? They can be so cute, if a little naughty, nê?

So, I don't suppose you want a swimming pool? But you would want a jungle . . . gym? With monkey bars, right? And, will you be needing a maid's quarters? Or will your wife's sister and your mother and your mother-in-law be living with you? Okay . . . okay, no problem, I've noted you want a swimming pool. [*Beat.*] Will you be keeping ducks?

What I mean, Mr Metaabeh, is, will you be keeping any animals? Goats, sheep, chickens . . . will you be doing any slaughtering? [*Beat.*]

Will you be doing any other monkey business? Like . . . running a shebeen, playing music out of the boot of your car, drinking in the driveway?

[*Laughs.*] Listen to me . . . just assuming things! Will you have a car? Or do you need to be close to public transport? [*Beat.*]

Off-street parking for three vehicles? Mr Maataabeh, if you're looking for something in a residential area, you won't be allowed to have a taxi rank in your driveway. [*Beat.*]

I'm just saying.

Do your monkeys speak English at home? No, I'm just thinking of schools. The suburbs we generally work in don't have schools that play football.

Okay, Mr Meetheeb, it sounds like you'd like to go. I'll get back to you . . . we don't have anything on our books right now that is what you are looking for, but give me your number . . . [*Doesn't actually write it down.*] 0-7-2 yes, 696-9002. Sure. Have a good day, and thank you for letting us be of service to you.

[*Puts the phone down.*] Maathabe. Meeteeba. Madiba! [*Snorts.*]

Sketch 9

SO-CALLEDS

The character is a 'so-called coloured' dude in his 50s, BERTIE. *He's having his hair cut by the barber,* JOE. *For the duration of the sketch his head is being shaven.*

BERTIE: Jirre, Joe, we bring up our laaities to think of themselves as South Africans, right? We think this population-group bullshit vrekked with those tricameral naaiers. But now every form our kids have to fill in . . . they get asked to fill in their race. I've told them to say 'one hundred metres'! This place is more race befok than when that poephol PW was waving his piel at us.

David's growing his Afro, getting in touch with his [*rolling his eyes*] inner black. He has to do this essay on 'white privilege' and how it impacts on [*wryly*] 'black pain'. He wants to know where *he* fits in.

In our day, Joe, we were all black. Now we are coloured. Not even so-called. Just . . . coloured. Biko would go fokken mal in this plek. We couldn't vote. They treated us all like gham! Okay, we didn't have to carry passes. And this was mos a preference employment area for us so-calleds! So we had privilege. And pain. But is anyone at UWC writing about this shit? My stirvy friends called it the University for Wasted Coloureds. [*Laughs.*]

Talking about wasted coloureds . . . you remember Roy September? Ja, that domkop who used to sit in the back of the class and try to fart 'Die Stem'. He's now a chief. Duidelik! He found out he has royal Griqua blood. [*Snorts.*] The only royal in his blood is the booze from the Royal Hotel, if you ask me! I said, 'Now that you're Griqua, no need to be Khoi, Roy.' [*Laughs at his own joke.*] Ag, I don't blame him. That's mos the system now . . . the bruin ous are learning from every Tom, Dick and Amandla who's getting appointed as chiefs, and then they all get a little plot of land and a vote-for-us stipend.

Maybe that's what that Oxford brat should do . . . the one who will only tip a white waitress when she gives back his land. [*Snorts.*] Bladdy hell,

Joe, if we only tipped people after we get back the things stolen from us, we would mos never tip coloured and black people! [*Shakes his head.*] Joe, you know I believe in anti-racism, but sometimes the kak in this country brings out the coloured in me. If it had been my daughter, I'm telling you, I'd kick that little fucker in his Oxford balls. Then all these popes of political correctness go on about how right he was. [*Posh-like.*] 'Because the land question has still not been resolved!'

Well, fuck that, Joe! Your family was moved from District Six. We were kicked out of Wynberg. I'm still angry, but it doesn't mean I have to be a shit human being, does it? But of course, these PC poephols will tell me that I [*feigning poshness*] 'can't tell anyone how to feel pain'. What do these spoilt fuckers know about detention without trial . . . about bloody torture?

A few weeks ago, I had a knock on my door. It was my white cousin from Joburg. Two of my father's brothers were mos classified white and they moved to Joburg. I haven't seen them since my ouballie's funeral 15 years ago. Now there's this white guy on my stoep in Penlyn Estate. He's fallen on hard times. Lost his job at Eskom to a black guy he was training. Then his wife left him.

Should I have chased him away? Shit, Joe, we're so busy with our pain porn or denying our privilege or trying to out-victim each other, we don't see people anymore! He's staying at our joint till he gets onto his feet. But I have chased my sister away from our house! She opens her bek and it's the kaffir government this, and the ANC kaffirs that! I told her to voetsek! Jislaaik, Joe, it would be really kwaai if government didn't feed these racists who think that all Africans are corrupt . . . or that blacks can't govern, hey?

I told you about Vuyo . . . Ndima . . . ja, the ou who was on the SRC with me at UWC. We spent four months in detention together and we became dik tjommies. I took my cousin to Vuyo's pozzie in Khayelitsha. It was the first time Vuyo had a white person in his joint . . . who wasn't a policeman. It was such a lekker evening . . . [*Beat.*]

It almost made me believe the rainbow nation was possible. [*Beat.*]

Can I ask you something, Joe? Have you ever had an African . . . you know what I mean . . . black people from the townships . . . have you ever had them in your house . . . for dinner or something? [*Joe responds by asking about his haircut.*] Ja, no, it looks nice . . . thanks. [*Wry smile.*] Nice and short.

Sketch 10

BLAME APARTHEID

The character is a singer named DÉJÀ VU.

DÉJÀ VU: Good evening. My name's Déjà Vu and I'll be singing 'Blame Apartheid'.

[*To the tune of 'That's Amore'.*]

When you don't get textbooks
When your leaders are crooks
Blame apartheid

When you're caught doing fraud
Or being drunk as a lord
Blame apartheid

When you're out of the team
Or out of ice-cream
Blame apartheid

When your statues must fall
If you're short and not tall
Blame apartheid

When you have stomach cramps
Or you're forced to use lamps
Blame apartheid

When you fail your exam
Or get chicken not lamb
Blame apartheid

For every thing
For the black quota wing
No BEE bling
Blame apartheid

If you must
For your lust
Even for a drug bust
Just . . .

[*Stops singing.*]

As audience supplies the last line and sings 'Blame apartheid', DÉJÀ VU
*stands with hands on hips, shaking his head. Then, when they stop, he
teases them.*

[*Sings.*]

When life throws a curve
We get what we deserve
If all we have is the 'blame game'.

Sketch 11

THE MET

The actor performs as a HORSE-RACING COMMENTATOR.

COMMENTATOR: There's a lot of excitement at the racetrack for this year's prestigious horse-race, the JHB Met! No, no, not the J&B Met that competes in the fashion stakes with the opening of Parliament, this is the five-yearly race for the Joburg Metro! The richest race in the country, the steaks are high and the gravy is rich. Till now, it has been pretty much a one-horse race, but load-shedding, service-shedding and moral-shedding have seen an opening up of the track, a more level playing field, a shifting of the goalposts . . . and a host of other political sporting clichés.

Still his own favourite, at 246 million to one, is Jacob Nkandla, riding his not-so-steady mare Pothole . . . a nightmare. Nevertheless, a well-hung stud . . . and that's just the jockey. Hold on . . . it looks like there's some discussion about whether he's a handicap or not, because next to him in the starting gate is Concourt Concourt, ridden by Moeng Moeng.

After losing the last race five years ago, Mmusi Obama rode off into the parliamentary sunset . . . clause, but like the unbroke . . . back man that he is, he's back on his high horse Let's Do It Like Cape Town!

Making his maiden entry in this year's race is Julius, riding his white horse . . . named Second Coming.

Joan Citizen will be riding that old chestnut Service Delivery, although, like Usain, it looks like that horse has bolted, and will be replaced by Protest Capital.

There are a few dark horses in the race . . . like Black Beauty. And White Fears. According to the touts, a good tip would be the filly Give Back Our Land.

This will be an August winter race, so with recent power outages, horse whisperers are expecting a dead heat.

[From this point, commentary is of the horse-racing variety.]

First out of the starting gates is Julius with full manifesto stadium, followed by Let's Do It Like Cape Town with voting fodder blue T-shirts on an open truck, and lying third, but lying regularly, is Jacob on Pothole, being chased down by Concourt Concourt. At the first turn is Cope, followed by Mmusi, who has been fast-tracked, and then comes Pothole shedding food parcels, now being chased by Second Coming with a bit in his mouth . . . pay back the money! On the backstretch, the two front-runners are neck and neck, but still below the 50 mark, and here comes Second Coming, it's Second Coming, Second Coming looks like the kingmaker, followed by Concourt Concourt, with Protest Capital making a run for it . . . this is exciting stuff . . . it's between Second Coming and Concourt Concourt, Second Coming and Concourt Concourt, with Protest Capital . . . it's Protest Capital . . . with 300 metres to go . . . [*excited*] . . . on the final bend . . . this is unbelievable . . .

Sketch 12

JULIUS

The character is JULIUS, *referencing Economic Freedom Fighters leader Julius Malema, who comments in Shakespearean style on the corruption and hypocrisy of the Zuma presidency.*

JULIUS: Friends [*rubs his tummy*], Romany Creams [*seriously*], Comrades and
    B-Com-rades!
    Lend me your jeers!
    For we have come to Parliament to bury Zuma
    Not to praise him!

    If music be the food of love, play on . . .
    [*Sings.*] Umshini wam, umshini wam . . . [*Stops abruptly.*]
    Enough! No more . . .
    'Tis not so sweet as it was before.

    To B-E-E or to G-U-P . . . T-A
    What a question!
    Zuma. Zupta. Guma.
    A crook by any other name is still a crook.

    He he he he he he he
    That strain again!
    It has a dying fall
    Just a matter of time
    Before a recall?

    That it has come to this
    There once was a time
    I would have killed for Zuma

    But now
    Beware the tides of march . . . ers
    As we descend upon Luthuli House

    [*Melodramatically.*] Not that I love Zuma less
    But that I love my country more.

[*Less poetic, bitter.*] Except for SARS of course
Bloody agents!

The course of true love never did run smooth

I once thought that Thabo had a mean and angry look
He thinks too much
Such men are dangerous
Clever blacks!

And now I see with Mbeki's ghost
The ghosts of hundreds of thousands of one-time believers
Spirited away on garlic and beetroot

Though we have buried Thabo
The evil that this man did lives after him
Resurrected each Monday in his Epistles of Denial

That I sometimes wish for his return
Shows how junk are the times we live in
But soft, soft . . . is this dagga I see before me?
Or is it a dagger?
Either way, I must be on the Cape Flats
Campaigning

Some are born great
Like me
Some achieve greatness
Like Khulubuse Zuma
Some have greatness [*pelvic thrust*] thrust upon them
How can we trust
A man who thrusts
And thrusts
And thrusts [*Beat.*]
And then takes a shower

A plague on him!

Point of order
Point of order

[*Conspiratorially.*] That lady . . . Mbete
She doth protest too much
Protecting Number One
While he lands us all in number two

Point of order!

Never did I believe that I would have to
Call so many honourable
Who bear that crown unworthily

Honourable Cyril
His hands still dripping miners' blood
Honourable Nhleko
Who believes in Father Christmas and firepools
Honourable Blade
Honourable Mthethwa
All like Brutus
Stabbing our people in the back!

But these are 'honourable' men and women
And it is *I* that must leave the Chamber!
Out! Out! Damned Julius!
I am a man more sinned against than sinning

Oh Fikile
Wherefore art thou Razzmatazz
Deny your Mercedes-Benz
Deny your Beyoncé concerts

Cross the floor!
It's not so cold outside!
The poor are dying
But ambition has hardened your heart

Yet all that glisters is not gold!
Fair is foul and foul is fair
But especially fair is the fowl from Nando's.
[*Holding his stomach.*] What pounds of flesh are these?
Agh . . . too much braai, too much beer, too much Kentucky.

If you prick us, do we not bleed?
And, if we go to Parliament,
Do we not get fat?

Life's but a walking shadow, a poor player
That struts and frets its hour upon the stage
And then is heard no more;

So bear with me just a little longer
Mine is a tale
Full of sound and fury,
Signifying . . . nothing

Or . . . so you would like to think.
And, with a wink
I thank you.

Sketch 13

RAINBOW SONG

The character is a singer named DÉJÀ VU.

DÉJÀ VU: Hello, my name's Déjà Vu, and I'll be doing the 'Rainbow' song.

[*To the tune of 'Over the Rainbow'.*]

Somewhere under the rainbow
Way down low
There's a land that all heard of
Where black and white were foes

Then, along came Madiba
From an island
And he made us a nation
With his magic wand

But then the rainbow came unstuck
The pot of gold was full of kak
Anger was fed
Both rich and poor were at their throats
Social grants bought many votes
Killed the rainbow dead

We're so over the rainbow
Nelson turns
Lying there six feet under
While the nation burns

The unemployed, the wretched poor
Are part of us and we of them
We need each other
But fear and ignorance, they rule
And hate and anger became cool
Dividing us

Daily under the rainbow
Harsh words fly
We don't know one another
And the rainbow dies

Sometimes I wish I were afar
Perhaps on Jupiter or Mars
By hook or fluke
Wherever there's no black and white
And all are green and there's no fight
On Facebook

The rainbow is so over
That dream's past
Only rich people thought that
This little dream would last

If only 'haves' may live and fly
All around the rainbow
Why, oh why, would I?

Lights down slightly to signal end of scene. Lights up.

Ladies and gentlemen, I'm pleased to announce that the time-travel machine has been repaired. Before we board and head back to the future, I'm going to have to ask you all to give us a little push to get it started . . . Thank you!

PLAY 5
STATE FRACTURE (2017)

Sketch 1

SAXONWOLD SHEBEEN

The character is a BARMAN *standing behind a well-stocked bar. He has an Indian accent.*

BARMAN: Hello, welcome to the Saxonwold shebeen. How may you help us? No, no, really, how may *you* help *us*? And then, we'll tell you how we can help you. We already have the president. The Indians have the chief, yes. We have the finance minister and half the cabinet. We have all the state-owned enterprises. We just need a bank. And now, maybe a few judges.

While you think about asking not what we can do for you . . . let me introduce you to our cocktail menu.

[*As if pointing to a blackboard behind him with the names written on them.*]

There's Sex on the Beach. Sex in a Mineshaft. Sex at Nkandla. Basically, we're happy for the South African taxpayer to be screwed anywhere.

We've got everyone's favourite, the Bloody Mary. Although we call it the Bloody Thuli. Same ingredients, but with a little bit of arsenic.

Then there's the Babalas Dlamini, after the Minister for Her Personal Welfare. [*Conspiratorially.*] You know, even *we* feel a little embarrassed by that one!

We have a special cocktail for students to honour their uprising, which, as you know, started with throwing shit at a statue – that's the Tequila Mocking Turd.

The Negroni is a mix of cheap darkies who will do whatever we want, and won't be shaken or stirred by things like . . . a constitution.

Besides the cocktails, we also serve Oros. I think he's over the age limit.

And we have some crafty beers!

There's the Lying Lager. If we get caught out, we just keep on lying.

We also have the Hansie Pilsner. That's the beer of the last resort – if our alternative facts don't work out and our emails are leaked, we just say 'the devil made us do it'. Apparently, the devil's not too happy with some of the things we do here.

Our premier league drinks are Ace Cider, Mabhuza Ale and Supra Brew! We have gin and tonic – here we just call it the Zille. She's not part of the premier league, but she may as well be. Very helpful to our faction.

Our good friend Brian Molefe has a cocktail in his honour; it's the Kamikaze. Brian put our shebeen on the map. We've become so popular, we've started a franchise in Dubai. Give that man a Bell . . . Pottinger!

Hey, everybody, all drinks are on the house! The House of Parliament!

Sketch 2

TRUMPLE-THIN-SKIN

This sketch is done in STORY-TELLER *mode, with the actor adopting different accents for the different characters, and employing direct audience engagement as if telling a children's story.*

STORY-TELLER: Gather around, boys and girls, moms and dads . . . the story I'm about to tell is . . . Trumple-Thin-Skin!

There once, not so long ago, in fact, right now, lived an orange monster, Trumple-Thin-Skin, with his 10-year-old son, his son's mother, and her Slovenian cat in a big, white house.

Starving after yet another day of pissing off Mexicans, Muslims and Melania, Trumple-Thin-Skin had started dinner with his son while his wife grated carrots for the daily salad. Trumple-Thin-Skin called to his wife, 'Melania, get your immigrant ass in here.' Melania came in from the kitchen with her back to Trumple-Thin-Skin, for she knew how he liked to grab her cat. [*Pause.*] [*Winks at the audience, then as an aside under his breath.*] This is a family show! 'Why does Trumple Junior have more peas than me?' shouted Trumple-Thin-Skin. 'Because you don't like peas, Trumple-Thin-Skin,' whimpered his wife as she placed the carrot salad on the table.

Trumple-Thin-Skin took his son's plate, scraped the peas onto his own plate, took a photo and posted it on Twitter. 'I have more peas than my son,' he announced to his millions of followers who re-pea-ted – or rather, retweeted – the picture 500 000 times.

'I know we've run out of T-rump steaks, but what's with the chicken? I asked for fish tonight!' sulked Trumple-Thin-Skin as he fed his son's peas to the dog. 'Well, someone issued an executive order saying "No more fishing in Yemen",' pleaded Melania, still shielding her Slovenian . . . cat from big Trumple-Thin-Skin's small hands.

Seething with anger, Trumple-Thin-Skin thundered, 'That is Hake News! I only banned people! Fish are not Muslim!'

With that he picked up the phone and called the chief of defence. 'General, I want you to send some marines to bomb the shit out of Yemen. [*Pause.*] What do you mean "why"? Because we can, dammit! And tell them to bring some fish back with them! [*Pause.*] No chips, just fish.'

You see, boys and girls . . . Trumple-Thin-Skin had more than enough chips . . . on both shoulders.

Trumple-Thin-Skin looked at the carrot salad with disdain. 'Melania! If I told you once, I've told you a thousand times, I want my carrots to be grated more finely than this! I promise you, Melania, I will make you grate again!'

It was at moments like these that their son knew he had to intervene to protect his mom. And her cat.

'Listen to that,' said Trumple Junior, pointing one of his 17 silver spoons at the window.

'Listen to what?' growled Trumple-Thin-Skin.

'The birds . . . they're tweeting.'

'What? What are they saying about me?' Trumple-Thin-Skin's hair turned a brighter shade of orange . . . as the carrot salad went to his head.

Just then, the head of the FBI – the Fake Bureau of Intelligence – walked into the dining room.

'Sir, we've received news that nude photographs of hundreds of female marines have been shared in a closed Facebook group.'

'That's terrible!' moaned Trumple-Thin-Skin. 'How am I going to look if it's a closed group?'

The FBI man smiled. 'We thought you might like to see them, sir, so we've brought a computer that has access.'

'I'm going to share these with my friend Vladimir,' grinned Trumple-Thin-Skin.

A little embarrassed, the FBI man responded, 'Actually, sir, we got these from Mr Putin. He hacked into the closed group. Sends his love, sir.'

Trumple-Thin-Skin got up. 'I need to go take a wiki-leak . . .' And with that he exited the dining room, through the kitchen, taking care to avoid the microwave oven, in case the former president was watching him.

'Where's Dad going with the laptop?' asked Trumple Junior. 'Is he going to grab himself again?'

Half-blind, but at least not physically challenged [*actor imitates disability that Trump mocked*], Trumple-Thin-Skin returned and settled down in front of Fox News to get his daily intelligence briefing. Just then, the phone rang.

It was the South African president. The laughing heyena wanted to talk to the orange monster about what do with judges who believed that *they* were running the country. 'That's why you need the CIA' was all Trumple-Thin-Skin would say, with a wink.

The phone rang again. Melania thought to herself, 'This is like living in an Obamacare call centre.'

It was the head of defence. 'Sir, I'm sorry to have to tell you that we lost a few marines in Yemen.' Trumple-Thin-Skin was like 'Yeah, yeah, whatever . . . did they get the fish?'

Disappointed, Trumple-Thin-Skin put down the phone and looked at his son. 'This guy is such a loser! Junior, do you want to be head of defence? I think you'd do a tremendous job. Tremendous!'

Before Trumple Junior could answer, Trumple-Thin-Skin's attention was captured by the alternative facts that kept rolling on the television screen.

The Mexicans had started to build a wall. The Saudis were funding it.

The Ku Klux Klan was experiencing a boom. As a charity organisation.

Trumple-Thin-Skin smiled as he tweeted: 'I kept my promise . . . we've taken our country back!'

He just forgot to say 'by seventy years'.

Sketch 3

CHICKEN SHITE

Actor is a female CHICKEN *in this sketch. Set this up – that is, chicken physicality – before speaking.*

CHICKEN: Some chicks have asked me how I came to be an egg-tivist. So I'm going to tell you. I was one of five chicks in our family, number three in the pecking order. My two brothers are autumn and my two sisters are winter . . . but I'm a spring chicken. My mother wanted me to be a poul-try dancer, but my father didn't think I had the legs.

My father was a comedian. He made yolks. About whites. He wasn't much of a rainbow chicken. He even roasted royalty . . . like chicken à la king. He ruffled a lot of feathers. But he brought us up to be streetwise. So that we could cross the road.

He had big dreams for us. He tried to hatch a plan so we could migrate to the Nkaaandla chicken run. Before he kicked the KFC bucket. The Nkaaandla chicken run is like the Australian chicken run. But for chickens. You can range freely there. Without the violence of lemon and herb or Colonel Sanders hanging over you.

We were very proud of our father. After he donated his organs to KFC [*muffled sob*], we heard that he was eaten by no less a person than Minister Bathabile Dlamini. [*Proud smile.*] She was celebrating the commission she got from Cash Paymaster Services. The company she tendered for Radical Egg-onomic Transformation. But now she has egg white on her face.

Anyway, my friend and I were watching this chick flick . . . *When Henny Met Cocky.* It was the usual American crap about a chick getting laid. But first they showed this ad about American chickens getting dumped here. Like we should be happy with these cheap, cheap chicks. I'm not xenophobic, but these chicks are taking our jobs. Our industry is losing jobs faster than the government loses court cases. Our free-trade chickens are coming home to roost.

So I decided to scratch a line in the sand.

I mean, these American chicks are pumped with salt water [*poses like a model*] to make them look good and soft. They live the life of brine . . . and then they come here to compete with us battery chicks! And they give off all kinds of diseases. Bird flu. Chicken pox. Even toothache. Chicken tand-oori.

We must resist! It doesn't matter if you are left wing or right wing. It doesn't matter whether your future is a nugget or a burger. This affects us all!

No to botox chicken!

No to chicken dumping!

Down with white-meat monopoly capital! Down!

Sketch 4

HELLO, LOOTERS

This sketch highlights 'state capture' by the Gupta brothers.

[*The song is sung to the tune of Leonard Cohen's 'Hallelujah'.*]

Our new country was doing okay
Then from the east, came Oakbay
We didn't know we entered a New Age
Atul, Ajay and Tony three
Brothers from overseas
Saw us as a bargain in Africa

Hello, looters
Hello, Guptas
Hello, Guptas
Hello, looters

Gigaba made them residents
So they could buy our president
And soon the country was up for sale
They sold off our democracy
Clothed them in hypocrisy
Said they were doing it for the poor

Hello, looters
Hello, Guptas
Hello, Guptas
Hello, looters

The brothers appointed our cabinet
And SOE boards, like Transnet
The ruling party watched this all go by
The money flowed
From the public purse
To Saxonwold and then much worse
Billions ended in Dubai

Goodbye, Guptas
Goodbye, looters
Goodbye, Guptas
Goodbye, looters

This song has been made possible by the sponsors of radical economic transformation.

Sketch 5

BLACKS ADOPTED BY WHITES ANONYMOUS

The character, LERATO, *is attending an AA-type support group. Actor speaks with a slight Afrikaans accent, mixed with a bit of an American twang.*

LERATO: Hello, my name's Lerato du Plessis, and this is my first time at BAWA. [*Wry smile.*] I'm not sure I like this acronym for Blacks Adopted by Whites Anonymous. Anyway, I'm 27 years old. I live in an apartment with my sister, Margot, in Rondebosch. She's two years older than me, and I have a brother, Hendrik, who's 32.

So . . . I'm here because last week, my mother came home from work, terribly upset. She works as a line manager in a financial institution and she'd just been charged with racism. The story as she tells it is that there's this young guy in her department, a black guy, who apparently has been sexually harassing a woman in the department. She's Kenyan and doesn't want to make a big thing of it because of this xenophobia thing and she doesn't want to bring attention to herself. My mom says this guy's quite a good worker; she likes him, he has lots of potential, so she sat him down and pointed out the potential consequences of his behaviour towards this woman. Nothing formal, just a motherly-type chat. I know . . . I've had a few of those! The next thing, he lays a formal charge of racism against my mother, accusing her of insulting his culture, of making out like he's a rapist just because he's black. Now *she's* been put on special leave till her disciplinary hearing in two weeks' time . . . but *he's* still at work!

I know I'm a cheesegirl, a coconut, whatever . . . but this kind of thing brings out the township in me. I want to go there with my brother and some of his rugby friends and stuff some Gorgonzola down this guy's throat!

To him, my mother's just another white woman in a country where it's just so easy to label someone a racist. For me, she's the only mother I've known. My granny worked for the Du Plessis family in Bellville for more than 30 years. My biological mother died when I was eight months old, and I became my granny's baby, so to speak. Magriet du Plessis offered to adopt me, which my granny was only too happy to accept. That was even before Nelson Mandela was released. I have only known love from this woman. I've been treated in the same way as my brother and sister . . . Hendrik dropped out of university, Margot is a graphic designer, and I'm . . . I'm the lawyer in the family. Listening to your stories . . . mine is a cliché. I wouldn't be what I am today without Magriet du Plessis. So for her to be accused of racism . . . [*Shakes her head.*]

Of course there's racism . . . ask me, I know. The things that Magriet has had to put up with from family and even church members because of me. She's never said it, but I know that her husband divorced her because he couldn't handle the social difficulties of having a black child. But with all this Facebook stuff . . . I sometimes feel like I'm living in that play, *The Crucible*, which we studied at school . . . Everyone's a witch! Everyone's a communist! Everyone's a racist!

Don't get me wrong. Racists need to be called out. But what gets me is how racism is used to cover up other evils. I know racism! But I also know what it's like to be 'fondled' by strange men in a taxi. I know about my comrades at varsity and their unwanted sexual advances! And I hate to think what would have happened to me when accosted by two guys in the township if my cousins hadn't intervened.

Black lives matter. For sure! But so do the lives of women! And the bodies of women! So before you go accusing my mother of racism, best you check your patriarchal privilege, dick!

Sketch 6

PASTOR HLAUDI, THE MIRACLE WORKER

The character is PASTOR HLAUDI, *addressing a congregation. Actor adopts an African American preaching style.*

PASTOR HLAUDI: Brothers and sisters-a, Pastor Hlaudi greets you all in the name of prosperity-a! For we did not join the SABC to be poor-a! No! We joined the SABC to work miracles-a! To be rich-a! To be like white people-a. And better-a!

For this is how we know we are blessed-a! We drive Mercedes-Benz-a! We have firepools-a! We get bonuses! Hallelujah! I said Hallelujah!

Brothers and sisters-a! The Gospel according to Jacob says that the ANC will rule until Jesus comes. He was a great man-a! He worked miracles-a! But let me remind you of the miracles that Pastor Hlaudi has done-a!

Jesus raised Lazarus from the dead-a. But me, Pastor Hlaudi-a, I raised my own salary-a! Other people need remuneration committees-a! They need board approval-a! They need ministerial confirmation-a! But me . . . I work a miracle-a! I . . . raise . . . my . . . own . . . salary! Amen!

They say Jesus made the blind to see-a. That, brothers and sisters-a, is easy-a! The SABC had a board-a. It had a blind chairman-a. Me, Pastor Hlaudi, I work a miracle-a! I made the blind to see even less-a! Praise the board-a! Praise the board!

Pastor Hlaudi also made those who see, not see! I worked a miracle-a! I made the news disappear-a! Any critique of our beloved president did not happen-a! Any violent protest-a, we made invisible-a! Any victory by the opposition . . . poof! This is the miracle of the SABC-a, the public broadcaster! Amen!

The Good Book tells us that Jesus turned water into wine-a! At the SABC, me, Pastor Hlaudi-a, the miracle worker-a, we turned whines into laughter! The DA took us to court-a! We laughed-a! The white press complained about us-a! We laughed-a! Parliament called us to account-a! We laughed-a! The more they whined, the more we laughed-a! For we knew from the Gospel according to Jacob that our time had not yet come! Hallelujah!

Jesus walked on water, and his disciples were amazed-a! Well, brothers and sisters-a, me, miracle worker Hlaudi-a, I did not just walk-a! I trampled! I said I stomped! Amen! I trampled on corporate governance-a! I trampled on Parliament-a! I trampled on the Constitution-a! That's me . . . Pastor Hlaudi!

They tell us that Jesus took two fish and five loaves of bread and fed 5 000 people! Brothers and sisters-a, me, the miracle worker, I fed lots of people, not just with Streetwise 2, but with KFC buckets-a! I said buckets-a! Amen!

The Bible teaches us that Jesus cast out many demons. Many, many, many demons-a! Brothers and sisters-a, I cast out many journalists from the SABC-a! Demonic people who spread lies-a! I threw them away . . . away with your anti-black news, you demons of white monopoly capital-a! Hallelujah!

Brothers and sisters-a, the devil comes in many guises. It could be some of your board members-a! It could be a parliamentary ad hoc committee-a! It could be the Constitutional Court-a. It is at times like these that you must bring out the Doom, brothers and sisters! It's time to spray! Spray, brothers and sisters-a, don't let the devil get you down! Doom the devil! I said Doom the devil! Amen!

People always say, 'Pastor Hlaudi is finished! He is over! He is dead!' But I showed you, I showed them-a, that I make the resurrection miracle! I have no matric, I get appointed chief executive. They make me leave this post-a, and I come back as chief operating officer-a. They force me out and say, 'At last, Hlaudi is dead,' but I come back as chief executive for corporate affairs! I am a resurrection miracle, brothers and sisters! Hallelujah!

To do this, you must have hope-a! You must have charity-a! But most of all, you must have faith-a! Faith Muthambi as the minister of communication-a!

The new SABC board tried sending me to hell-a. They make me fired-a! But they forget, I am 90 per cent South African and 100 per cent Zuluboy-a! Like the Terminator, Pastor Hlaudi will be back! Amen! Hallelujah!

Sketch 7

ABBA MEDLEY

In this sketch a singer performs a medley highlighting various themes and inci-dents. 'Money, Money, Money' is about corruption; 'Fernando' is about the lack of safety against criminals while politicians have VIP protection; and 'Waterkloof' is about the Guptas landing their wedding plane at Waterkloof, a national key point.

[*Sings to the tune of 'Money, Money, Money'.*]

A tender here, a backhand there
We loot, we steal, without a care
Don't get mad
It's our turn at feeding troughs
For too long we've had it rough
Once were rad

Now we don't care for the mentally ill
The old, the poor, are expendable
We take, we eat, what we can
We just don't give a damn

Money, money, money
Milk and honey
It's a quick-rich world
Sunny, sunny, sunny
Always sunny
In our quick-rich world

Aha Aha

All the things we could do
If we had all that money
Stolen, wasted
In this quick-rich world

It's the turn of blacks to be rich
Stop your whining, don't you bitch

For you had
Once you stole and now it's time
For us to steal, and it's no crime
We ain't bad

In our fight we did not plan
To be poor like every man
It's only for us few
We've been around, but this is new

Money, money, money
Milk and honey
It's a quick-rich world
Sunny, sunny, sunny
Always sunny
In our quick-rich world

Aha Aha

All the things we could do
If we had all that money
Stolen, wasted
In this quick-rich world

[*Segues into 'Fernando'.*]

Have you heard the guns, Fernando?
There was screaming, there were shots, a bullet to the head
Have you heard the mums, Fernando?
There was weeping, wailing, for another son is dead
You can hear this every night and every day
And every day, we wish it'd go away

There shall be security
And peace for all
So they said
Then they drive around with bodyguards
And blue-light cars
To Nando's

Criminals they rule our streets
They rule our lives
If I had to vote again, for repeats
I won't, my friend, Fernando

Even if we vote again, my friend
This won't end, Fernando.

[*Segues into 'Waterloo'.*]

Why, why, at Waterkloof, the Guptas landed their big plane
Oh yeah, I had to take the fall but it was not in vain
As history books always tell
We always look after ourselves

Waterkloof, I took the fall for Number One
Waterkloof, he said I would find a place in the sun
Waterkloof, knowing my fate is to be with him
Waterkloof, finally it would be win-win

My, my, I tried to hold you back but you were stronger
My, my, I tried to keep my pride but he was stronger
Oh yeah, and then it seemed my best chance was not to fight
And how could I ever refuse
I feel like I win when I lose

Waterkloof, I took the fall for Number One
Waterkloof, he said I would find a place in the sun
Waterkloof, promoted to be an ambassador
Waterkloof, Holland calls for three years or more
Whoa, whoa, whoa, whoa
Waterkloof, Holland calls for three years or more.

[*Speaks.*]

But where's the sun?

Sketch 8

SOME BLACK LIVES MATTER

The character is a POET, *performing on stage at a poetry festival.*

POET: Thank you for inviting me to the annual Thabo Mbeki African Renaissance Irony Poetry Festival. I'll be reciting the poem 'Some Black Lives Matter'.

Hey brother mine
When next you decry those Afro-pessimists
Or reach for your 'blame apartheid' card
Or feign victim hurt for what colonialists wrought
Remember this day, the day of Goodwill, your king

Activist you
When next you petition me to march
Behind your banner declaring 'black lives matter'
Because some African American's been shot
Remember this day, as I turn and walk away

And you, you braided Model C poet
With your naïve Mother Africa poems
Drowning in a river of Congo blood
I vomit at your impotent words

As for you, taxman
When next you tax me another Madiba statue
Whose 'never and never again' echoes hollow
Across this murderous land
I shall be first to tear it down

You better-lives-for-some
When you have done with your semantic dance of denial
Spare me your empty ubuntu bullshit
Save me from your social cohesion crap
It is a necklace burning our Zimbabwean
Mozambican

Somalian
Neighbours that speaks for you

You so-called leaders
Whose sons grow fat on African mines
Whose daughters parade their African art
Whose spouses bedeck your tables with African cloth
While you serve African bodies on skewers of hate

Here
Take my passport
Its pages are full
They are stamped with shame

Sketch 9

STAND-UP ON PRIVILEGE

The character is a stand-up comedian, NKOSINATHI MXENGE.

NKOSINATHI: Thank you, thank you very much! A big shout-out to Ricky Cohen, ladies and gentlemen! For an emerging comedian, it's a great opportunity to be invited to do the opening act for a stand-up like Ricky! My name's Nkosinathi Mxenge but you can call me Friday. It's really cool to be with you in the suburbs tonight. I'm planning on leaving here without becoming a poster boy for Black Lives Matter, so, if you can play along, that will be great.

I'm privileged to be with you in the suburbs . . . see how easy it was for me to say 'I'm privileged'? I'm fascinated by how privileged people deny they are privileged. So in the five minutes Ricky has given me to piss you off, I thought I'd spell out privilege for you. It's P-R-I-V-I-L-E-J. Privilej . . .

'P' is for professional networks. I was amazed at how easy it was for Ricky to pull off this gig tonight. His aunt runs the catering company. His stepmother's in PR and a school buddy owns the venue. Even the bouncers are the cousins of his stepmom's Congolese gardener. Where I come from, we also have professional networks, but we call them gangs.

'R' . . . 'R' *has* to be for race, right? It took Ricky five minutes to emerge on the stand-up scene, and another 10 minutes to have his own radio slot! We're the same age, but I'm in my third year of 'emerging'. I'm hoping to graduate at the end of this year. And then there are people who tell me that race doesn't exist; it's just a social construct! Yeah, right! It's already taken me three years to get over an obstacle that doesn't exist.

Earlier today, I was in Sea Point, and so enjoyed the view of the sea, the people walking along the promenade, white people picking up their dogs' shit. I was in Ricky's flat. Which his grandparents left him. So 'I' is for inheritance. Imagine having that kind of head-start in life. It's like being in a 100-metre race with Usain Bolt, but you're starting at the 400-metre mark. When my dad died, my three sisters and I shared what was left of his funeral policy. We were so happy to have a smiley and a Coke.

'V' is for vasectomy. It has nothing to do with privilege, but it's such a cool word which I came across when I was trying to find out how to spell privilege, I had to use it in my show. Vasectomy. Just imagine where we would be as a country today if Jacob's dad had had a vasectomy. *Before* Jacob was born. But he was too busy being a policeman protecting your inheritance from the disinherited to learn big words about small snips. The 'V' in privilege is actually for vegetarian. White folk actually have a choice about what they'll eat. They can be Banting-tarians, vegetarians, Presbyterians. That, people, is privilege!

There's a second 'I' in privilege . . . for individual. For white people, it's all about number one! Every cent that Ricky will earn from this gig will go into his bank account. Okay, maybe a bit to his dealer. For us, anyone who earns money is like an ATM. Palimony on behalf of your unemployed uncle. School fees for your second cousin twice removed. A donation to your sister's weave. The black tax! Eish! So I've asked Ricky to pay me in book vouchers. My people don't read.

The 'L' in privilege could be for land. But you got that point under inheritance, right? So 'L' is for language. White folk don't know just how privileged they are! The world works in their language. That's why it's taken me so long to emerge. I've had to coconut my accent. Cheeseboy my split infinitives. And learn to spell so that I can make white people laugh in my third language! And make sure they're not laughing *at* me!

Which brings me to 'E' for education. We all laugh at how Jacob struggles with numbers. And we cringe when he assaults his speeches. But just imagine if the same money had been spent educating black children as on white kids. We wouldn't have to import Zimbabweans to make up our racial quotas. Everyone in Ricky's family went to varsity. I'm the first in ours. Now here I am, Ricky's 15 per cent BVE partner . . . Book Voucher Empowerment partner.

'G' is for God. Despite what many of you might believe, I'm sorry to break it to you, but you don't have what you have because God blessed you. Unless you see Cecil John Rhodes, Verwoerd and Botha as the trinity. You have privilege because you gave black people your God, and made them believe that they don't need land on earth, because they'll have mansions in heaven. While white people have heaven on earth.

So what's the second 'E' in privilege for? It's the economy, stupid! Like Ricky, I own my means of comedic production, as my sociology lecturers would have said. But my people have some way to go before they own the venues and the radio stations to distribute my work. And it's going to be a while before they have disposable income on the scale I need to sustain the lifestyle to which Ricky has made me accustomed. [*Ironically.*] Which is why I have to subject myself to the violence of white laughter. Ouch!

Enjoy your privilege while you can! P-R-I-V-I-L-E-J. The 'J' is a heads-up that J is coming . . . no, no, not Jesus . . . Julius!

Thank you . . . while I slip out the back door.

Sketch 10

THE HELEN ZILLE SCHOOL OF GOOD COLONIALISM

The sketch references Helen Zille's social media tweet maintaining that not everything about colonialism was bad.

Dear Subscriber

Thank you for registering for the Helen Zille School of Good Colonialism. Please note that this course may only be taken online, and is conducted in 10 lessons of 140 characters, plus or minus.

Lesson One.

Thanks to colonisation, you have the wheel. Without the wheel, where would Winne Mandela have been with only a box of matches?

Lesson Two.

Colonialists brought the Bible. Without Christianity, Jesus would not return. And the ANC would rule forever. So thank God for colonialism.

Lesson Three.

It was Europeans who brought you guns. And cars. Without us, you would still be hijacking horse-riders with spears.

Lesson Four.

Remember who brought you democracy? If it were not for colonisation, you would not have the Parliamentary Channel.

Lesson Five.

Why did the chicken cross the road? To escape brutal Stone Age slaughter for the more humane deaths offered by colonial machinery and electricity. This, before being delivered to you as Nando's or KFC.

Lesson Six.

Colonialism brought slaves. Without slaves, there would be no coloured people. And we would not have Jonathan Butler, the Kaapse Klopse and the gatsby.

Lesson Seven.

Colonialism brought Dutch. And English. And Malaysian. So today, we have Afrikaans. And Steve Hofmeyr. But because of English, everyone can now support Manchester United.

Speaking of which . . .

Lesson Eight.

Without colonisation, there would be no soccer. So yes, you can blame Bafana Bafana on us.

Lesson Nine.

Without colonialism, you would not have tarred roads. At least not until the Chinese arrived. And without tarred roads, you couldn't have blue-light brigades. Just saying.

Lesson Ten.

I admit, not all of colonialism was a great experience for the locals. And I apologise for the bad stuff. But we have more than made up for it by giving you Johnnie Walker Blue. Golf. Flat-screen TVs. And Panado.

Which brings me to Lesson Eleven. A free lesson for having been through the first ten lessons.

Don't be a twit. Twink before you tweet.

Sketch 11

SOCIAL COHESION

The sketch deals with racism between 'coloured' and 'black African' communities. There are three distinct 'voices': the DIRECTOR and the two young actors playing the Shakespearean characters ROMEO and JULIET.

DIRECTOR [*addressing audience*]: Twenty-three years into the rainbow nation, our country is still torn apart by racism. So to build social cohesion, the Department of Arts and Culture is sponsoring a production of *Romeo and Juliet* on the Cape Flats. Romeo is played by Sandile Ndebele from Pinelands, and Laetitia Abrahams from Manenberg plays Juliet. We invite you to a rehearsal of the play.

ROMEO [*African accent with a hint of Model C schooling, only a slight touch of campiness*]: But soft! What light through yonder window breaks?

JULIET [*heavy Cape Flats accent*]: Daddy, Romeo says there's some laaitie breaking in through the window.

ROMEO: It is the east, and Juliet is the sun.

JULIET: Juliet is the daughter, Romeo, the bladdy daughter! Jirre! This is not your moffie play.

ROMEO: Arise, fair sun, and kill the envious moon,

Who is already sick and pale with grief,

That thou her maid art far more fair than she:

Be not her maid, since she is envious;

It is my lady, O, it is my love!

O that she knew she were!

She speaks, yet she says nothing: what of that?

JULIET: What do you want me to say after all that kak that just came out of your mouth?

ROMEO: She speaks:

O, speak again, bright angel! for thou art

As glorious to this night

As is a winged messenger of heaven

JULIET: Romeo, Romeo! wherefore the fok art thou, Romeo?

    I would that you were Alpha

    Then you could be Alpha Romeo

    Love that car! [*Snorts.*]

ROMEO: What? Sweet lady?

JULIET: Deny your father . . .

ROMEO: Laetitia, that's my line . . .

JULIET [*strongly*]: I put it to you, your father's a naai . . . !

ROMEO: Yes, my lady.

JULIET: So, refuse your name;

    Or, if thou wilt not, be but sworn my love,

    And I'll no longer be a Cap-in-hand

    No longer not white enough for the past

    Nor not black enough for the future

    But coloured enough for this play

ROMEO: 'Tis but my name that is thy enemy?

JULIET: No, it's your colour too. If my brothers and cousins saw you here, they'll

    moer you!

ROMEO: What's in a name?

    That which we call a rose

    By any other name would smell as sweet

JULIET: Maybe for you, because you live in Pinelands, Romeo!

    Here in Manenberg, this is Daffodil Close

    Over there is Marigold Avenue

    And to the back is Tulip Street

    They all smell like piss

    And even if I change all their names to Nelson Mandela Boulevard

    Or Patricia de Lille Drive

    Or even Rose Crescent

    They will all still smell like piss.

ROMEO: I take thee at thy word:

    Call me but love, and I'll be new baptised;

    Henceforth I never will be Romeo.

JULIET: I know where you're going with this.

> You say you love me across the colour line
>
> Across the clothes line
>
> But I think you just don't want to pay lobola for a black chick.

ROMEO [*to the director; that is, towards audience*]: Can't I rather do this with a white actress? This is really difficult.

DIRECTOR: The department has given us the money to address racism between blacks and coloureds. So, I'm afraid we just have to do this.

ROMEO: This is a tragedy.

DIRECTOR: Yes, one of Shakespeare's finest. Now, let's continue towards the tragic end.

JULIET: Romeo, Romeo, wherefore art thou such a wus?

ROMEO: Sticks and stones may break my bones

> But names will never hurt me.

JULIET: Oh ja? And if my father and brothers call you the 'K' word?

ROMEO: Kickback?

JULIET: No!

ROMEO: Kibbutz?

JULIET [*shaking her head*]: Do you want to call a friend?

ROMEO: Kinky?

JULIET: Kardashian!

ROMEO [*falling apart*]: Okay, this is getting ridiculous.

> Mixing art with reality.
>
> And then with reality TV!
>
> Let me be saved from this insane world
>
> Here's to my true love
>
> Willem Ackerman
>
> O true apothecary
>
> Thy drugs are quick
>
> Thus with a kiss I die.

JULIET [*to director*]: You still want me to kiss him?

> I mean, you heard him . . . his true love is Willem!
>
> He was on drugs . . . maybe antiretrovirals.
>
> What if he had AIDS?
>
> I'm not going to kiss him.

And anyway, why should I die too?
Where's the hope?
At least if I'm alive
There's a future.
Maybe I'll meet a German . . .

Sketch 12

SOCIAL MEDIA ROLLERCOASTER

The aim of this sketch is to show how divided middle-class South Africans – those linked by social media (Twitter, Facebook) – are when it comes to uniting around strategies to achieve – probably – common goals. It is in the form of a rollercoaster ride, with the actor going up when things appear to be good (unity), followed by swift declines and sharp twists and turns when there are divisions. At the end, there is no unity, and we only hear Zuma's laughter as the sketch fades.

There is the option for the words to be recorded and the actor to play them out as if sitting on a rollercoaster; or the actor can recite the words and perform at the same time.

ANNOUNCER: Welcome aboard the Unity-in-Diversity, Disunity-in-Adversity Rollercoaster. To pay, simply click on your Facebook or Twitter account. Remember to fasten your seat belt.

[*Actor crouches and slowly ascends as if the rollercoaster is moving slowly upwards towards its start.*]

[*UP*] [*Ascends and speaks slowly initially, getting more and more excited.*]

Unemployment Must Fall
Crime Must Fall
Rhodes Must Fall
Fees Must Fall
Zuma Must Fall
Guptas Must Fall

[*Sharp down.*]

Why only Zuma?
Why not Zille?
Top six must go
ANC backed Zuma
Call election
And after Zuma?

[*Abrupt stop, then smooth, gentle ride.*]

Pravin
Pravin Gordhan
Vote Pravin
Pravin Support Group
Pravin Gordhan for President

[*Sharp swerve left.*]

Pravin fronts white monopoly capital

[*Sharp swerve right.*]

Pravin's a communist

[*Sharp swerve left.*]

Pravin's a neo-liberal

[*Sharp swerve right.*]

Pravin voted Zuma

[*UP*]

He's not Zulu

[*DOWN*]

He's Indian

[*UP*]

He's honest

[*Goes progressively down.*]

Shaik is Indian
Guptas are Indian
I don't trust Indians

[*Swerve left.*]

I don't trust Zulus

[*Swerve right.*]

They're better than whites

[*Swerve left.*]

What about Trevor?

[*Swerve right.*]

He married white capital

Recorded Zuma laugh: Hehehehehehe.

[*Actor hears laughter; slow ascent upwards.*]

We must do something
We must unite
Work together
Wear black on Monday
March on Tuesday
Petition on Wednesday
Go to court on Thursday
Stayaway Friday

[*As if riding on a really bumpy road.*]

I can't march with capital
Call when you march for jobs
You only march when the rand goes down
Why march on Luthuli House?
Let's march to the Guptas
I'll join when whites march to give back our land

Recorded Zuma laugh gets louder, longer: Hehehehehehe.

[*Actor gets more anxious; ascends again.*]

Defend the Constitution
Protect our Democracy
Save our Country

[*Straight and relatively calm.*]

Let's Occupy

Tahrir Square
South Korea
Burkina Faso
All ousted presidents

[*UP*]

I'll follow on Facebook

[*DOWN*]

What if it rains?

[*UP*]

I'll donate a tent

[*DOWN*]

The police will shoot

[*UP*]

I'll bake a cake

[*DOWN*]

Recorded Zuma laugh plays under the next lines.

I've got book club
Is it legal?
I don't have transport
I'm watching football
Will my car be safe?

Lights fade as actor's voice gets softer and softer and Zuma laugh builds to a crescendo.

Sketch 13

THE PATRIOT

This sketch highlights the attempts by politicians and their supporters to silence criticism by name-calling. For maximum effect, it is to be performed with as little movement as possible, with the performer looking the audience in the eye, firmly but not arrogantly.

I am not a patriot
For pointing out naked emperors
For not joining the chorus of praise singers
For allegiance to country, not party

I am anti-transformation
For still sprouting non-racist mantra
For resisting cadre deployment
Choosing delivery not patronage

I am a sell-out
For donating my poetry to resistance
For refusing to live in denial
For declining 30 pieces of silver

I am an ultra-leftist
For supporting human rights in Zimbabwe
For not being a millionaire socialist
For saying what others but think

I am a racist
For breaking the silence with a whisper
For preferring thought to propaganda
For standing up amidst the prostrate
For repeated conspiracy with the questions what, how, why

I am a white monopoly capitalist
For marching against corruption
For not looting the people's purse
Choosing principle above expedience

I am a counter-revolutionary
An enemy of the people
An agent of imperialism
An apartheid spy
A traitor
For not martyring my mind
For not holding my tongue
For not sacrificing my soul

I have been here before
But then as a communist
Marxist
Terrorist

Labels they come and labels they go
Hard on the footsteps of those
Who defend new privilege with old morality
Who appropriate history for contemporary pillaging
Who now crucify the people on their electoral crosses

I have been here before and I shall be here again
For as long as the poor – like Truth – are with us

Sketch 14

NO ZUMA, NO CRY

This song highlights the corruption allegations against former president Zuma while expressing hope for the future.

[*To the tune of Bob Marley's 'No Woman, No Cry'.*]

No Zuma, no cry
No Gutpa, no cry
No Zupta, no cry
No Guma, no cry

Sad, sad, sad I remember
When they used to sit
In Parliament in Cape Town
They made us all a constitution
That shone light for all the people, yeah
Good hope we had, good hope we have lost along the way, yeah
For our great future was hijacked by the thieves
But dry your tears I say

No Zuma, no cry
No Gutpa, no cry
No Zupta, no cry
No Guma, no cry

Do you remember
The promises they made
To serve the people not one man
But what they've done, this ruling party, yeah
Is sell our dreams, and auction the nation
But now we're rising, we're saying it's gone too far, yeah
We're taking back the future, kicking out the thieves
We know no fear, I say

Everything's gonna be all right
Everything's gonna be all right

Everything's gonna be all right
Everything's gonna be all right
Everything's gonna be all right, yeah

Get up! Stand up! Don't give up the fight!

Blackout.

PLAY 6
LAND ACTS (2018)

Sketch 1

DERYA HANEKOM

The character, DERYA HANEKOM *– a play on 'Derek Hanekom', who was the minister of tourism, and who was fired by President Zuma – is a tour guide addressing a group of visitors to South Africa.*

DERYA: Good afternoon. I'd like to welcome you to South Africa on behalf of the Big Five and our president, who together make the Top Six. President RamaPoser wanted our finance minister to meet you, but I put up my hand and said 'Send me!' My name's Derya Hanekom and I'll be your guide during your stay in our beautiful country. If I'm not available, then one of my [*grits teeth*] sleeping [*normal*] partners in Rainbow Nation Tours – Loshni Naidoo, Rosie September or Moses . . . will stand in for me.

I trust you all had a good flight? Yes, we are aware that it takes two days to get through passport control, but if you decide to invest in our country, the minister of home affairs can arrange a South African passport for you. Even two.

Please accept this little gift from the minister; it is the feather of our national bird, the ostrich. We also have an international bird . . . and, dear investor, it . . . is . . . YOU! You are our golden geese who will lay your investment eggs that will hatch lots of jobs.

Some of you have been asking about expropriation without compensation, and whether your investment will be safe . . . [*Pause.*] Are there any other questions?

[*As if listening to a question.*] Yes, you *will* get to see the Big Five. In fact, we have a herd of white elephants . . . FIFA football stadiums. They gave birth to an elephant in the room; we promised our people houses, but we gave them . . . football. We don't have any more young lions; they have all become fat cats. You will see a leopard at Nkandla; he's no longer the president, but he hasn't changed his spots. Despite the poaching, we do have black and white rhino, but the bruin ou is still under threat . . . not white enough for the past, not black enough to name an airport after. Shame.

[*Responding to another question.*] Yes, we are thinking of doing a township tour. In fact, we wanted to correct apartheid's spatial geographies as a priority, but then we realised how popular the township tours are with tourists, so we've decided to keep the townships.

Some tourists don't feel safe in the townships, so now we are thinking of bringing the township to you. Instead of you going to look at people in the township, they will come to look at you. Township residents will have two minutes to tell you their story before moving on to the next tourist. If you are moved by anyone's story, you can empower them with $5, which includes Rainbow Nation Tours' facilitation fee.

[*Listening to another question.*] Definitely yes, we are going to take the cable car up Table Mountain. And yes, it is safe. According to police statistics, it's the only kind of car that hasn't been hijacked yet. Although the police have warned that the cable could be stolen at any time.

We will also be going to Kirstenbosch, where we're busy with a project to get rid of all the aliens. From the continent. But we really hope that you investors from around the world will stay.

Please follow my brolly and stay close together to make it easy for the police to protect you. Just so you know, the guys in blue with the automatic rifles are the police. And the guys in brown with the panic buttons are the private security firm, hired to protect the police.

Follow me!

Sketch 2

GIVE ME A SIGN, JULIUS

The character is a young, woke black woman. She could be exercising, running, or doing yoga or Pilates. The reference is to Julius Malema, leader of the EFF, at Winnie Mandela's funeral, calling on 'Mama' to give them a sign to act.

YOUNG WOMAN: Hey, Julius, what's with all this 'give back the land' bullshit? I'll tell you this for free: red's not my colour. And berets and overalls? That's so . . . '60s! You want my vote in 2019? Then give me a sign, Julius.

I didn't get a master's degree in economics so I could grow cabbages. And the other women who got degrees – before you got yours – they are also here. We want to be pilots. Lawyers. Astronauts. Run our own companies. So give us a sign, Julius. It doesn't have to be a Seeff sign. Or Pam Golding saying 'SOLD'. It can say 'EXPROPRIATED'. With or without compensation. We're cool with that.

If you and your boys want to do the whole farmer, patriarchal, boer-maak-'n-plan thing with your [*sexual innuendo*] sprinklers and fertiliser, go right ahead. But the women who wear kangas? They are also here. We don't do 'Boer Soek 'n Vrou'. Or 'There's a Zulu on My Koek'. We swipe right when we want. Because we can! We're lit. We're woke. Our clits. Unyoked. We got your sign, Julius! And we don't need your breakfast. Or your taxi money!

Thandi Modise . . . she gave us a sign, Julius. With her pig cannibals eating other pigs at the trough! Like the revolution eating its children. You can keep your one-man-one-goat! You want to give us land? Speak to the hand! We want two-bedroomed apartments. En suite. With a shower for the drought. And a bath for when it rains. And a sea view. With a lock-up garage. For a car, a scooter and a stand-up paddle-board.

The wheat-frees, the low-glutens and the lactose-intolerant are also here, Julius. Mornings are for gym. For Pilates. Yoga. Not for pulling on Daisy's tits. If we *want* milk, we go shopping. Give us a sign, Julius! 'WOOLIES . . . THIS WAY'.

The women who listen to music? They are also here. We would rather listen to The Soil than work it. And the book clubs are here, Julius. We read Chimamanda Adichie. Zuki Wanner. NoViolet Bulawayo. We. Don't. Read. Farmers. Weekly. Ever. We Netflix. Spotify. Instagram. We don't need land . . . lines! We saw the sign . . . TELKOM. And we said, No thanks!

I know you don't care much for the rainbow sign, Julius. Frankly, neither do I. But I'm turned on by the thought of a white PA making me black tea, with one brown sugar. I don't want to grow the tea, Julius! Nor the sugar! I just want to taste it! And give a white boy a job. And save him from the genocide against white farmers, shem! [*Snorts.*]

I must say . . . I admire your farming, Julius. Sowing a little chaos. Reaping a lot of headlines. Incubating those smallanyana ANC chickens. Letting them come home to roost as the EFF. And those cash crops. But then, you had a lot of signs. Signed tenders. Signed procurements. Signed cheques.

By the way, the girls love your Land . . . Rover. Probably given to you for your birthday, so SARS doesn't get too upset? You're a Pisces, but the other signs are also here. Gemini, Scorpio, even Virgos. We don't do blessers, Julius! 'Cos we got the power!

Good luck with your land . . . slide!

Sketch 3

MIDDLE FINGER FOR THE NATIVES

The character is a COWBOY *with a 'Western' drawl.*

COWBOY *enters leading his horse. Stops. Holds his hand above his brow.*

COWBOY: What a fine piece of land I've just discovered [*pats horse*], Dromedaris. [*Makes an approving neigh sound.*] Yeah, I'm glad you like it too! All the way up the mountain, down to the river, and along the seashore. So lush. So beautiful. So . . . mine!

[*Mounts horse and rides in a circle. Stops, reverses.*] Whoa! There's a savage on our land.

[*Addressing someone.*] Hey, boy, you speak English? Good! So you got yourself some civilisation. What's your name, boy? [*Person doesn't understand;* COWBOY *acts out patronising/racist.*] What . . . your . . . momma . . . call . . . you? [*Pause.*] Matanzima Mangope Buthelezi? [*Snorts.*] What kinda name is that, boy? From now on, your name is Tonto. [*Pause.*] [*Laughs.*] No, not Toronto! That's the name my cousins gave the capital of the land *they* discovered! From now on, you ride with me. Well, when I get you a horse. Till then, you run with me. My name's Billy Abraham Andrew Shackleton . . . but you can call me BAAS for short.

[*Looks perturbed.*] What's that noise, Tonto? [*Looks around.*] Oh no! More savages! Hundreds of them! [*Takes out his rifle and stands at the ready.*]

What they saying, Tonto? [*Listens to Tonto.*] Say what? This is *your* land?

[COWBOY *shoots. Gives the impression of many machine-gun-like shots.*]

Your land? Not any more it ain't. C'mon, Tonto . . . leave them bodies to fatten up those vultures.

[*As he gallops.*] Where did you learn English, Tonto? Missionaries? Good on them . . . preparing the way for civilisation to reach the undiscovered world. And where are the missionaries now? [*Nearly falls off his horse.*] They got eaten? [*Pause.*] Tonto, you don't have a taste for white meat, do you? [*Pause.*] Good! [*Pause, as he thinks about how to make a deal to keep Tonto in check.*]

Tonto, you see that piece of land up the mountain? You can have that. [*Pause.*] No, no, not the forests and the waterfall, you big tease, you! There . . . with all the lovely rocks and the sunshine. You can live there with whoever else works for me. Okay?

Right, since there are no more missionary positions, I guess I'll just have to educate you myself! Time to learn the alphabet, Tonto!

'A' is for Adam, the first man God made in his image. And he was white! Like me. And God said: 'Adam . . . see all this land and stuff like the savages I made? I give it all to you to rule over.'

Which brings me to 'B' for Bible and the two most important commandments: 'Thou shalt not steal!' and 'Thou shalt not kill!' No more killing white people, Tonto! That's 'G' for genocide! And we don't do genocide! And no need to steal from me! I've given you some land.

Civilisation. That's what 'C' is for. Enlightenment. Progress. Development. And piped water. Just like Mrs Zille says.

'D' . . . 'D' is for democracy. Now you're not ready for that yet. So in the meantime, we white folk will get to choose who rules over you lot.

'E' is for education. But you won't be needing much of that. 'Cos you going to be hewers of wood and drawers of water. Just like the Bible says.

'F' is for freedom. But no need to be learning about that either.

'H' is for human rights. But to have them, you have to be human, right?

I forgot about 'G'. 'G' is for gold. As soon as I discover where you guys have found it, Tonto, you can bring all your other cousins to work for me.

But 'G' is also for gin. And 'T' is for tonic. Time for gin and tonic, Tonto! But also time for you to work my land. And remind all your half-breeds to come to church on Sunday!

Or me and my whip will give them 'H' for hell on Monday.

Sketch 4

MACDONALD'S FARM

This song speaks to government inaction on land reform, even while many leading politicians have farms.

[*To the tune of the children's song 'Old MacDonald Had a Farm'.*]

Old MacDonald had a farm
E-I-E-I-O
But burgers make him wealthy now
E-I-E-I-O
With a Big Mac here
French fries there
Here's a beef, there's a chick
Everywhere a double thick
Old MacDonald's on a high
M-O-N-E-Y

Old MacVorster bought his farm
R-A-N-D-S
But on his farm he caught bird flu
H-5-N-1-nest
A dead fowl here
A dead fowl there
Here's a fowl, there's a fowl
Everywhere a dying fowl
Old MacVorster sold his farm
Willing seller he

So the state bought his farm
Willing buyer they
They sat on it for years and years
In fact, right to this day
With a land claim here
And a land claim there
Here's a claim, there's a claim
Everywhere's a land claim

Now the state still owns the farm
Yippee-doodle-do

Young MacPhosa bought a farm
B-U-F-L-O
And on his farm he had a herd
B-U-F-L-O
Ten million here
Ten million there
Here's a turd, there's a turd
Everywhere's a buff'lo turd
Young MacPhosa had a farm
Thank double-U-M-C

Half the cabinet has a farm
Viva ANC
Their voters got their promises
Viva RDP
A matchbox here
A matchbox there
Here's a box, there's a box
Everywhere a township box
All the cabinet had two homes
Time for R-E-T.

Sketch 5

A PROMISE FULFILLED

The character is a POET, *performing on stage at a poetry festival.*

POET: Thank you for the invitation to appear again at the Thabo Mbeki Annual African Renaissance Poetry Festival. This poem is called 'A Promise Fulfilled'.

The plots are marked
Or most of them
Their waiting lists need
No councillor bribe
No backhander pay-off
No party gift
Nor application form
Demanding race
Though 'black' will be unspoken firsts

Age matters not
Here young and old
Even the unborn
Are eligible

A place to visit
For families to remember
The good times
To share a laugh
Some rehearsed story maybe
And then a mournful
Shake-of-the-head

New neighbours arrive daily
Random selection outsourced
To the grinning reaper
By official neglect

Harvested by
Disease

Taxis
Knives
Guns
The favoured scythes
To take up their promise of land

Two feet wide
Eight feet long
Six feet deep

Hundreds
Thousands
Even millions

Promised in their lifetime
Bestowed in their premature deaths

A plot of land for all

Sketch 6

CAR GUARD

The character is a CAR GUARD *hanging around on a street, helping drivers to park and assuring them that he'll keep an eye on their cars until they return.*

CAR GUARD [*singing to the tune of Ladysmith Black Mambazo's 'Homeless'*]:
Homeless, homeless
At night we sleeping on the bench again
Harmless, harmless
We also want our sun to shine again

[*Sees a car in need of parking.*]

Hello, sir, here's a lekker bay
Have a lekker day

[*Under his breath.*] And perhaps a lekker vry

[*Turns his attention in the opposite direction.*]

Madam, I look nicely after your car
While you're in the Spar
Or maybe in the bar [*Snorts.*]
No, the nails bar, madam

You want a car wash, my lady?

No, my lady, I know there's a drought. But me and my friends, we do a spit wash. Ja, we spit on your car and then . . . [*The lady has said no thank you.*]

What a stirvy goose! [*To audience.*] On a Sunday, she and her friends have a spit roast, but on a Monday, too stirvy to have a spit wash! Probably from Fairways. [*Turns his attention to a car.*]

Hello, my lanie, anything for the shelter

No need to skel, sir

[*Under his breath.*] Oh, go to hell, sir

[*And then, as if after the guy has turned his back on him.*]

Don't be surprised by the scratch on your car, sir

[*At audience.*] Only joking.

But I'm sure that's what many of you think, nê? 'I better be nice to the car guard, or next thing I'll have a nail in my tyre, or he'll do graffiti on my bonnet!' So I just want to put this out there . . . we are car guards, not a protection racket. Well, most of us. Actually, I can only speak for myself. I don't speak French.

Look, let's be honest. If you are anything like I was before I fell on hard times, you are irritated by car guards. Either they're waving you into a space which you spotted yourself; or you never see them, until you're getting into your car and they come running from a kilometre away, saying 'Everything's fine . . . your car is safe'. Like they had anything to do with it.

CAR GUARD's *phone buzzes.*

[*To audience.*] Sorry, just hold that thought. [*He types a message into his phone.*] I run a business on the side. Uber Trolleys. There are so many of us living on the streets now, but not everyone has to steal, I mean, borrow a shopping trolley anymore. You can now order an Uber Trolley from me. We have different kinds of trolleys. We have the more expensive Trolley W, that's the one from Woolworths, if you want to look through Camps Bay bins on Tuesdays. Then there's the Checkers trolley . . . Trolley C . . . for places like Claremont and Rondebosch. And then we've got the Spar trolleys – Trolley S – for anywhere else. Like Kalk Bay. [*Or wherever the sketch is being performed at the time.*] However, we don't go into areas like Manenberg. And Nyanga.

Dogs have kennels, bicycles have lanes and cars got parking garages and bays. But the City doesn't care about those of us who live on the streets. They just show us their gat. In fact, we call it 'The City that Twerks for You'. [*Twerks, bursts out laughing.*] But we're doing it for ourselves . . . very entrepreneurial. Many of us have a favourite place . . . underneath a bridge, on a shop stoep, or a bench on the Promenade if you want to wake up with a sea view. But sometimes we get enough money for the shelter, and it's nice to have a real bed to sleep in. Then we Airbnb our bench or our stoep. Through the grapevine, if you know what I mean.

We could just beg and ask you for money. But you'll think . . . 'He's going to spend it on drink again' or 'Why doesn't he get a job?' So this is why we offer this service . . . to guard your car . . . which you don't really need. We have more dignity this way, and you feel a little better about parting with a tiny percentage of what you just spent at the restaurant.

So, no need to hug your car guard . . . just a nice tip would help keep us off your stoep.

[*Sings/hums, transitioning to next sketch.*]

Homeless, homeless
At night we sleeping on the bench again
Harmless, harmless
We also want our sun to shine again

Sketch 7

AUSTRALIAN REFUGE

The character is an ABORIGINAL AUSTRALIAN.

ABORIGINAL AUSTRALIAN: On behalf of the Aboriginal and Torres Strait Islander people, I would like to apologise to South Africans for the cricket ball-tampering incident.

Unfortunately, we are not surprised by this kind of cheating. Steve Smith and his fellow Gubbas were only trying to steal a cricket match. In our case, they not only took all our wickets, so to speak; these full tosses also forcibly stole – not a run or two – but generations of our children. This happened till 1970, when Australia played a test series in South Africa for the last time before that country was banned from international cricket. Because of apartheid, a crime against humanity. [*Snorts.*] Australia should have been banned for 50, no, for centuries before that, given their crimes against us. Little wonder we are now less than 4 per cent of the population.

Maybe that's why we're not in the cricket team; there's not enough of us. Or maybe it's because they're scared that if we throw in the ball from the boundary, it will boomerang back to us. How's that? [*A look of incredulousness.*]

The Ozzie prime minister says it's unbelievable that the cricket team should be caught cheating. 'They've always been associated with fair play,' he says. Yeah right, with the emphasis [*pointing to his skin*] on 'fair'. He wants the Cricket Board to come down on the culprits with a sledging hammer.

Well, what about reparations for our land? For our stolen children?

So we got a declaration. From a former prime minister in 2008, apologising for the stolen generation. We have a National Sorry Day – 26 May; it's supposed to be a day of healing, building from 'the ashes' of the past. But it's been a real slog . . . 10 years on, the scoring has been slow.

At least some white folk now acknowledge the crimes of the past. At the beginning of events, they get to say things like 'We acknowledge the

Aboriginal and Torres Strait Islander people as the original inhabitants of this continent. We recognise their loss of land, children, health and kin, and the erosion of their languages, culture and lore, and the manifold impacts of colonisation.' I smile when I think about white South Africans in denial about their past, who now have to make this acknowledgement here in their adopted country.

Here's something our government can do for us. By doing something for black South Africans. We know about genocide so we have a duty to help those facing it.

There were 19 000 murders in South Africa last year – that's an average of 52 every day. Seventy-four of those took place on farms. It took a year to murder as many people on farms as are murdered in one and a half days in the black townships. It's safer for black South Africans to live on farms . . . even though a third of those killed on farms are black. But after 24 years of democracy, black people still don't have land.

So we appeal to the Australian government: help black South Africans to escape the genocide, and to resettle here!

Maybe then we'll also have a black person in the national cricket team.

Sketch 8

A DOG'S LIFE

In this sketch, the actor plays a pampered DOG, *commenting on the fear of many South Africans of what land reform will mean for them.*

DOG: Woof! [*Trying to get an audience reaction.*] WOOF! You people like to say 'It's a dog's life'. Like we spend the whole day lying in the sun. Licking our balls. And chasing cats. [*Pause.*] Well . . . some days the sun doesn't shine. Just saying.

And now with everyone barking about expropriation without compensation, it looks like what's left of my dog's life is coming to an end. Next thing, Beauty will be sleeping *inside*, and *I'll* be out on the stoep!

The other day, I took Beauty for a walk . . . her real name's not Beauty, but we call her that to make her feel better about her life. Shame. Anyway, I had to keep her on a tight leash, because every time she saw another domestic, she was like 'Wakanda, Wakanda'. Crossing herself like a Christian expecting a mansion in heaven. Because of the first coming of Julius.

We don't really get along . . . Beauty and me. We may both be black, but that's where it ends. First, I'm a dog. Man's best friend. She's just . . . black. Second, she doesn't have matric. I went to a Model C dog school. As you can hear from my accent. [*Barks 'upper class'.*] Third, I get to have the leftovers from the family table. Which is why it pisses me off when she clears the table and eats some of *my* food before feeding me. She says the family doesn't want a heavy pet. Thinks she's funny.

So every time she puts more than two sugars in her tea, or stuffs a toilet roll in her bag to take home with her over weekends, I bark like hell. And when she steals my food, I make the biggest turd outside her room. It's like the turd world war.

Which is why when they take over, I think Beauty will be quite happy to dump me in a township. Have you seen those township dogs? Once those undernourished tsotsi dogs see me, it will be dog eat dog!

Last week, I went to see *Hair, the Musical* . . . starring the usual Siberian huskies and golden retrievers. The show got cancelled because the lead couldn't keep his paws off the lead-ess! Hashtag MeToo! The entertainment industry's full of it!

Anyway, we all landed up at the Bark Inn and there was a lot of bitching . . . not about the show being cancelled, but about what's going to happen when *they* take over. Everyone was hot under the collar. One fleabag said he heard that we were all going to be exported to China as food. That made the sausage dog burst into tears . . . we always teased her about being a hot dog. She first thought we meant she was sexy. Someone said the Chinese are already here . . . we're being flooded by Pekingese. The English mastiffs and Yorkshire terriers are not worried . . . they already have their British passports. The Afghan hound reckons that whatever happens, it will still be better than where he's from. The bulldog was typically dogmatic . . . he's not going anywhere! Nearly got into a fight with the boxer who said he's talking a lot of bull. For a dog. Even Rover and Jock interrupted their usual argument about which was better, Rolex or Tag Heuer – they were both good watch dogs. This little yapper was going on and on about the tail wagging the dog, about the EFF dictating ANC policy. As Julius would say, bloody chihuahua!

But everyone's scared. We can see [*lifts his leg*] the pissing on the wall. The days of dog privilege are soon going to be over.

I get on very well with the family except Merlin, who's in Grade 9. Always blames me for eating his homework. It took me a long time to forgive them for neutering me . . . they said they didn't want me to litter. They've been good to me since, but I know that when the shoe hits the turd, they'll be out of here, and I'll be left behind. With Beauty.

So I'm thinking of leaving the country before things get bad. Two poodles have invited me to Malta. They are South African poodles, but their great-granny is Maltese.

I'm just waiting to be vetted . . .

Sketch 9

WHAT A WONDERFUL WORLD

This song comments ironically about the frustrated hopes of the 'rainbow nation'.

[To the tune of 'What a Wonderful World', made famous by Louis Armstrong.]

The hills of KwaZulu
The open Karoo
The luscious Limpopo
Please not Limpoo
And I think to myself
What a beautiful world

I see Madiba statues
I saw Rhodes fall
Orania koeksiesters
Monuments all
And I said to myself
What a colourful world

I hear politicians
Deciding our fate
I see social media
Stirring up hate
So many out there, shaking their fists
There's no more rainbow, only thick mist

First there's a drought
And then there's rain
I hope for healing
After the pain

For I think to myself
We've a bountiful world
Yes, I think we all know
We've a bountiful world

I see mansions large
In suburbs green
And shanty towns
With deadened dreams
And I think to myself
Unsustainable world

If we are human
Then let's agree
This can't continue
This cannot be

I see many fake chiefs
Now claiming land
And I see good people
Drawing lines in the sand
So many out there, shaking their fists
There's no more rainbow, only thick mist

If we are human
Then let's agree
This can't continue
This cannot be

Let's think for ourselves
Save our beautiful world
Yes, let's think for ourselves
And save our beautiful world

Sketch 10

SHAKESPEARE IN LOVE

Actor uses an English accent to play a modern-day SHAKESPEARE *speaking to an estate agent. The conceit is a use of many Shakespeare play titles and a sprinkling of quotes throughout the monologue.*

SHAKESPEARE: Hello, the name's Shakespeare. William Shakespeare. I'm in love . . . with your country. Well, I'm more out of love with mine. I'm doing a Brexit . . . in reverse. I believe you have very fine actors here, and they're cheap! So I'm thinking of making my work here, tour the world in dollars, and pay the actors in rands. Writing is so much easier these days on my *Macbeth* Pro. So yes, I'd like to buy – not a whole village – just a little *Hamlet*, if I may.

I would need a place with a garage for two cars. I have a *Troilus and* a *Cressida*. They are being shipped over by a friend of mine. He's a *Merchant* in *Venice*. I flew over in my *Lear*, so if I could also have a bit of runway, that would be splendid.

My partner, Dick, was supposed to fly over with me, but he got stuck in *Coriol's anus* with a bout of *Titus Andronicus*. Too much information, I know, but it was a real *Comedy of Errors*. After the *Twelfth Night*, I said *Richard, the Second* you get unstuck, please join me. I have to go, or my special skills permit may run out. But *All's Well That Ends Well* and Dick is on his way.

No, I don't mind who I have for neighbours, as long as it's not *Henry V* . . . Henri van Breda.

[*Looking at a catalogue of houses.*] Ah yes, these places look lovely, and I could also have a six-roomed cottage at the sea. My girlfriends – Desdemona, Juliet and Cleopatra – I call them *The Merry Wives of Win* Some, Lose Some – Desdemona and Juliet would love to do a house swop. If they're still around. You know how it is with intimate partners nowadays.

I didn't expect it to be so . . . chilly. It will warm up soon? So I suppose I'm getting *Winter's Tale*? I am looking forward to *Midsummer Night's Dream*s under the African stars.

Tell me, I met these *Two Gentlemen from Verona* in the airport lounge . . . apparently they've decided to leave South Africa because of this *Tempest* about the land . . . is it serious, or *Much Ado About Nothing*? If my land, this blessed plot, this earth, this realm, this little piece of England does get taken . . . I'd like at least *Measure for Measure* in compensation.

I could pay by EFF . . . sorry, EFT or cash or swipe my card . . . Just *As You Like It*.

But tell me . . . will my *Hamlet* be safe, or will *Julius Seize* it?

[*Pause.*]

[*Smiles.*] You're not just saying that . . . like 'Trust me . . . I'm an estate agent', you *Shrew*, you!

Sketch 11

ODE TO WANKANDLA

In this sketch a POET *comments on the extravagant and illegal expenditure of public funds on President Zuma's private home.*

POET: This poem is an ode to WaNkandla.

When the corruption bells first rang their wail
They were dismissed as Western conceit
'Typical Afro-pessimists'
They jeered
'With no understanding of our culture'

Then when next the whistles blew
They were cold-shouldered as white racism
'Where were your voices when apartheid
Corruptly favoured whites?' they hurled
'You just don't want blacks to be rich!'
When they full knew of many among them
Whom whites had made more wealthy than even wealthy whites
To laager white wealth

When exposé after exposé exposed the rot
They were rebuffed as sensational media
Journalists were agents of monopoly capital
Defenders of minority privilege

As the anti-looting volume grew louder
It was pooh-poohed as middle-class concerns
Typical parliamentary opposition
Seeking electoral advantage

Then when party veterans raised their hands
And even the communists raised their voice
At last to defend the poor
When party branches raised their fists
In anger at a president captured for treasonous ends

They were reprimanded as undisciplined
Acting outside the party culture

When courts put a halt to new looting schemes
To stop the assault on the country's crippled vaults
They turned their venom on the Constitution's defenders
'Who are these unelected men and women
Who dare think they run the country?
Clever blacks who should be thankful
For what this government had allowed them to become.'
And then they helped themselves to millions more
To appeal for their right to ill-gotten gain

Then when black masses marched
When blue and red walked side by side
And left and right found common cause
The thieves
Their fake prophets
And their rented shirts
Assumed the radical position
Their rhetoric about
Land and
Economic transformation
Echoing hollow over
The country's sucked-dry coffers

By the time it was all over
There was little left to steal
Only a people divided
By crooks
Who had long robbed their own conscience
And auctioned this to foreign bidders

That it has come to this

Sketch 12

FOOTBALL MATCH

The character is a FOOTBALL COMMENTATOR.

COMMENTATOR: Welcome, listeners, to today's match, where the political
football is . . . land. In the last match, the political football was Zuma, with
the opposition winning handsomely, mainly through the ANC scoring
numerous own goals. They didn't want to know their backhand from their
handball.

The ANC – the green team – has a new captain, but to keep his team
together, he has kept some terribly out-of-form and politically injured
players in their positions.

Once more, the ANC is both player and referee. They have also bought,
sorry, brought the lines-people who will determine who's offside and
who's not.

The game kicks off. The red team passes the land resolution to the green
team. The green team passes the buck, sorry, the ball to its national
working committee. The working committee stabs it through to the
national executive committee. The national executive committee lobs the
ball to the top six. The top six heads the ball to a land summit.

The blue team intercepts the ball. The red team appeals for offside, and the
referee blows his whistle on the blue team. Patricia de Lille cheers from
the stands.

The green goalkeeper prepares to take the free kick. He pulls up his
socks. He ties his shoelaces. He runs up and then . . . he stops. He looks
around . . .

Julius complains that the goalkeeper's wasting time. The referee
yellow-cards the goalkeeper, and now all the goalkeeper needs is the race
card to complete the ANC's colours.

The goalkeeper kicks the ball into touch, high into the stands. The crowd
catches the ball and refuses to let it go. The police are sent to get the ball.

The crowd sets up barricades. They burn tyres. The police open fire. Fourteen people die and 63 are injured. Israel withdraws their ambassador in protest. The police manage to retrieve the ball.

It's a throw-in to the blue team. Steenhuizen to Selfe. Selfe to Zille. Zille to Trollip. Mmusi – their centre front, sorry, their centre forward – is screaming for the ball, but it's a one-two-one-two between the old boys. And girls.

The spectators in the boxes are urging their team on. The boxes are reserved for 20 per cent of the spectators who earn 70 per cent of the national income.

Eventually Mmusi gets the ball just outside the box, but he is tackled from behind by three players in red shirts. Mmusi the diva dives. But no penalty, as the foul happened outside the box. Meanwhile, many in the green team are eating the fowl in the KFC box. Which makes the 20 per cent spectators in the boxes very cross, as they are the ones paying for the fowls in the box.

The green and red teams form a wall. Mmusi prepares to take the kick, but Steenhuizen sends him to the far post. Steenhuizen shoots, and it comes off a green defender. It's a corner to the blue team. The spectators outside the boxes are calling for social housing, but blue team members bid for the corner. And now the winner is building a luxury high-rise apartment block.

We have a bit of a hold-up; there seems to be some problem in the green team. There are two or three women players who look very unhappy. Danny Jordaan says he has nothing to do with it.

The ball is back in play. Supra from the Premier League has the ball. He passes to his son. His son passes to Magashule's son. Magashule's son passes to Mabuza's son. Mabuza's son looks around to pass to Duduzane, Jacob's son . . .

The red team are shifting the goalposts, bringing them closer together to make it easier to score. The blue team are consulting their lawyers . . . they want someone on the bench to save them.

The red team has been red-carded, and they are being forced off the field. Their fans are throwing bottles onto the pitch. The referee is appealing for calm. He is offering a minimum wage, but the spectators keep booing.

The ordinary spectators are invading the pitch. The police have rushed to the boxes to protect the 20 per cent spectators, who are now being escorted to their Ubers. Spectators are digging up the pitch and taking pieces with them. Others are building shacks, occupying large parts of the field.

It doesn't look like play will resume tonight. So we cross back to the studio for our game show. Over to Nick and Naas for *Pick Your Plaas*.

Sketch 13

IMAGINE

This song expresses hope for a future in which poverty and inequality are no more.

[*To the tune of 'Imagine' by John Lennon.*]

Imagine we're in heaven
A decent house for all
No more hell and brimstone
Around us no more walls

Imagine all our people, living in harmony

Imagine there's no poverty
Will be hard to do
No more theft and break-ins
No more killings too

Imagine all our people, living life in peace
You . . .

You may say I'm a dreamer
But I'm not the only one
I hope each day more will join us
And we all can live as one

Imagine no armed response
No electric walls
No one will sleep hungry
A nation caring for all

Imagine all our people, sharing in our land

Imagine life without fear
Seeing each other's eyes
Hate and anger banished
All breaking into smiles

Imagine all our people, living as humans should
You . . .

You may say I'm a dreamer
But I'm not the only one
I hope each day more will join us
And we all can live as one

You may say I'm a dreamer
But I'm not the only one
I hope each day more will join us
And we all can live as one